HARV

In Other
WORDS

A DEVOTIONAL GUIDE

TATE PUBLISHING
AND ENTERPRISES, LLC

This book is designed to provide accurate and authoritative information with regard to the subject matter covered. This information is given with the understanding that neither the author nor Tate Publishing, LLC is engaged in rendering legal, professional advice. Since the details of your situation are fact dependent, you should additionally seek the services of a competent professional.

The opinions expressed by the author are not necessarily those of Tate Publishing, LLC.

Published by Tate Publishing & Enterprises, LLC
127 E. Trade Center Terrace | Mustang, Oklahoma 73064 USA
1.888.361.9473 | www.tatepublishing.com

Tate Publishing is committed to excellence in the publishing industry. The company reflects the philosophy established by the founders, based on Psalm 68:11,
"The Lord gave the word and great was the company of those who published it."

Published in the United States of America

ISBN: 978-1-68333-291-6
Religion / Christian Life / Devotional
16.06.10

Dedication

Shadrach, Meshach, and Abednego are some of my heroes. Daniel 3 tells about a time when King Nebuchadnezzar constructed a ninety-foot-tall and nine-foot-wide statue. All who approached the statue were to bow down and worship the image. Shadrach, Meshach, and Abednego refused to bow. Nebuchadnezzar found out that they were not bowing. He had them brought to him. He had the furnace heated seven times more than usual and threatened to throw them in if they didn't obey.

> Shadrach, Meshach, and Abed-Nego answered and said to the king, "O Nebuchadnezzar, we have no need to answer you in this matter.
>
> "If that is the case, our God whom we serve is able to deliver us from the burning fiery furnace, and He will deliver us from your hand, O king.

"But if not, let it be known to you, O king, that we do not serve your gods, nor will we worship the gold image which you have set up." (Dan. 3:16–18, NKJV)

What is heroic is the simple statement "But if not." God is able to deliver us, but even if he does not, it doesn't matter. We will still serve him.

This book is dedicated to those who have made my life fuller, have lifted me up and increased my faith, and said, "God will deliver me, but if not…"

To Bruce C., Karen and Volley H., the Camp Verde 14, Richard and Annette H.

To Lonnie G., Larry D., Dave and Edie A., Dave and Bonnie C.

Contents

Foreword

In Other Words is an introduction to a restatement of what has already been said. For Christians, the basis of our beliefs and lifestyle is the Bible. Pastors encourage us to read it regularly and apply it to our lives. Psalm 119:9–11 says, "How can a young person stay on the path of purity? By living according to your word. I seek you with all my heart; do not let me stray from your commands. I have hidden your word in my heart that I might not sin against you."

Harvey Shapiro has taken several key passages from the Bible and has restated the concepts that help the meaning come alive for our generation and culture. Through these pages, you will also get to know Harvey. One of his characters is Hershel, the Jew. I wonder how he is related to Harvey. Harvey was born into a practicing Jewish family.

Prayer is very important to Harvey. He started a Sunday morning prayer group at our church for the purpose of asking

God's blessing and protection for everything that happens on that Sunday morning. As you read Harvey's *In Other Words*, concerning the Lord's Prayer, you will learn that God's name is actually Howard. As a boy who lived in Connecticut was heard praying, "Our Father which art in New Haven, Howard is Thy name." Combine this sense of humor with a person who grew up in a Jewish home treating God's name with overwhelming respect and holiness, and you have Harvey Shapiro.

Harvey's theological background is in the Wesleyan-holiness tradition. He brings his unique style to the subject of sanctification and titles one of his devotionals, "Sanctification—What It Ain't," and lists nine "falsehoods" or misunderstandings. This section could be a classic of theological literature.

I have been Harvey's friend for fifteen years, and his pastor for eight years. I wish I had known him in his younger days, in the 1970s when he sported a bright orange afro hairstyle and ran a camera shop that developed film the old-fashioned way. Somewhere along the way, God reached this Jewish free spirit and transformed his life. For two decades, Harvey combined his Jewish background, his incredibly bright mind, his knowledge of the Bible and Christianity, and his love for people, into a great pastor. Those who listened to him preach regularly were incredibly blessed. Parkinson's disease forced Harvey into early retirement. Watching Harvey battle this debilitating disease is an inspiration. In spite of the disease,

Harvey leads a Sunday school class, teaches ministerial-studies classes in an online format, writes devotionals like the one you are about to read, counsels and encourages many who are going through struggles in their lives, and thinks up all kinds of inventions that could make life easier. While I enjoy Harvey's friendship here and now, I can't wait to be around Harvey in heaven, where he will be free from the limitations of disease.

This book is not meant to be read in one sitting. Take your time. Read a chapter at a time, and savor the concepts. May the Bible, and the God of the Bible, come alive for you in your daily life, which is what Harvey intended all along.

—Bob Ogden
Pastor, Peoria Church of the Nazarene
Peoria, Arizona

The Lord's (Disciples') Prayer
Our Father Art

THIS IS AN in-depth view of the Lord's Prayer. It should really be called the Disciples' Prayer as Jesus did not sin; He had no reason to ask for forgiveness. The real Lord's Prayer is found in John 17, and not in Matthew 6:9–15.

> "This, then, is how you should pray: 'Our Father in heaven, hallowed be your name, your kingdom come, your will be done on earth as it is in heaven.
>
> Give us today our daily bread.
>
> Forgive us our debts, as we also have forgiven our debtors.
>
> And lead us not into temptation, but deliver us from the evil one. For thine is the kingdom, and the power, and the glory forever. Amen.'" (Matt. 6:9–13, NIV)

The prayer only contains sixty-six (66) words, forty-four (44) of which have only one syllable and takes only about thirty seconds to read aloud. It is simple and short yet comprehensive and profound. That's how most of Jesus's teachings were, simple yet profound.

> "Art doesn't listen to me—it's no use." The boy sighed with sadness and disappointment.
> His mom asked, "Art who?"
> The boy responded with disgust, "Art in heaven."

Maybe you have felt like the atheist. You call Dial-a-Prayer, and no one answered.

We must remember that we are praying to a father and not a force. To a loving father and not some aloof being.

Jesus modeled an intimacy with the Father that was unknown among the Jews. They considered themselves as servants of God but not His children. They believed in Him and feared Him but never knew the joy of intimacy with Him.

In praying to God our Father, we find that He is near to us and not distant. It is like the songwriter said, "He's as close as the mention of His name."

Our prayers are so important to Him that, according to the book of Revelation, He pours them over the altar in heaven—they are like sweet incense to Him.

Referring to God as *Father* can be and is a problem to many due to their bad earthly fathers. Many see God as a strict, harsh father. One who has a clipboard and marks down everything that we have done wrong. It is hard for some to believe in a Heavenly Father who loves them, and yet that is what God is—love.

When we pray "Our Father," we are acknowledging that we are part of the family of God. Our Father cares about each one of His family members. He is not some busy CEO who is hidden by a wall of secretaries. I have always thought of Jeremiah 33:3 as, in a sense, His phone number: "Call to me and I'll answer you."

His line is never busy. He doesn't have some computerized switchboard saying, "You have reached the office of God. He is either away from his desk or is on the other line. If you wish him to return your call, press 1 for healing, 2 for miracles, 3 for wisdom, 4 for…"

He is always nearby, ready to hear our prayer. A little girl prayed, "Our Father who art in heaven, how do you know my name?"

God does know our name and cares about us. The God of love welcomes us and understands us even more than a loving earthly father. Can you grasp it? The God of the Universe, the Great I Am, the King of Kings, the Lord of Lords, the Alpha and the Omega, the Beginning and the End calls us his kids. The word *Abba* really translates as "daddy." Imagine calling God daddy. Because he loves us and calls us his children, we can.

> How great is the love the Father has lavished on us,
> that we should be called children of God! And that is
> what we are! (1 John 3:1, NIV)

What a wonderful Father, our Father Art.

Part 1: Howard Is His Name

A boy who lived in Connecticut was heard paying: "Our Father which art in New Haven, Howard is Thy name." Most of us learned to say this prayer in the King James Version of the Bible and have never really considered what the phrase "hallowed be thy name" means. It is not another one of his names. What the words are meant to do is to paint a strong picture of admiration for God.

Have you ever closely examined the prayer? When we do, we see that there is an order to it.

1. We begin by acknowledging that God is our Father.
2. Next we hallow [praise His Name].
3. Then we ask for His will to be done.
4. Next we are to ask Him to provide our needs.
5. We next ask for forgiveness.
6. We finally ask for strength to avoid sin.

By calling Him Father and hallowing His name, we are putting Him first.

The word *hallowed* means "devoted to sacred purposes." In other words, holy.

In Hebrew school, I was taught that God's name is so holy that any reference to God must be written as G-d.

Exodus 19 emphasizes the Holiness of God by giving us an interesting scene.

> And the Lord said to Moses, "Go to the people and consecrate them today and tomorrow. Have them wash their clothes and be ready by the third day, because on that day the Lord will come down on Mount Sinai in the sight of all the people. Put limits for the people around the mountain and tell them, 'Be careful that you do not go up the mountain or touch the foot of it. Whoever touches the mountain shall surely be put to death. He shall surely be stoned or shot with arrows; not a hand is to be laid on him. Whether man or animal, he shall not be permitted to live.' Only when the ram's horn sounds a long blast may they go up to the mountain." On the morning of the third day there was thunder and lightning, with a thick cloud over the mountain, and a very loud trumpet blast. Everyone in the camp trembled. Then Moses led the people out of the camp to meet with God, and they stood at the foot of the mountain. Mount Sinai was covered with smoke, because the Lord descended on it in fire. The smoke billowed up from it like smoke from a furnace, the whole mountain trembled violently, and the sound of the trumpet grew louder and louder. Then Moses

spoke and the voice of God answered him. (Exod. 19:10–13)

Can you image being there and experiencing this scene firsthand? What a frightening time. They couldn't even touch the mountain without the fear of being killed. Call God our Father? No way. A God who would kill you for getting too close. I'm to call Him my Father?

> They were completely unnerved by the divine edict that "If so much as a beast touches the mountain, it shall be stoned to death." They knew that if it meant death to a dumb, uncomprehending animal, how much more surely would it mean death to those who understood the warning. The entire scene was so terrifying and forbidding that Moses himself was trembling. All this speaks eloquently of the nature and ministry of the law. It is a revelation of God's righteous requirements and of His wrath against sin. The purpose of the law was not to provide the knowledge of salvation but to produce the knowledge of sin. It speaks of distance between God and man because of sin. It is a ministry of condemnation, darkness, and gloom. (William MacDonald and Arthur Farstad, *Believer's Bible Commentary: Old and New Testaments*; Nashville: Thomas Nelson, 1997)

Before we get too depressed, let's look at Hebrews 12:18–24.

You have not come to a mountain that cannot be touched and that is burning with fire; to darkness, gloom and storm; to a trumpet blast or to such a voice speaking words that those who heard it begged that no further word be spoken to them, because they could not bear what was commanded: "If even an animal touches the mountain, it must be stoned." The sight was so terrifying that Moses said, "I am trembling with fear." But you have come to Mount Zion, to the heavenly Jerusalem, the city of the living God. You have come to thousands upon thousands of angels in joyful assembly, to the church of the firstborn, whose names are written in heaven. You have come to God, the judge of all men, to the spirits of righteous men made perfect, to Jesus the mediator of a new covenant, and to the sprinkled blood that speaks a better word than the blood of Abel.

Because of the shed blood of Jesus and His death and resurrection, we no longer have any reason to fear. We can now approach the throne of God boldly. We can touch His holy mountain without fear. No longer is there condemnation and gloom and fear. We can get close to God. We can even call him Father and acknowledge His holiness. He can even call us holy. Isn't that wonderful? He calls us to be holy and provides the way and the means!

Our father Art who lives in heaven Howard is his name.

Part 2: Give and Forgive

Give us today our daily bread.
And forgive us our debts,
As we also have forgiven our debtors

This looks like a pretty cut and dry easy part of the prayer. However, when we begin to take a closer look at it, we will see that this may be the most difficult part. It is not as difficult as a lawyer made it:

> We respectfully petition, request and entreat Thou Almighty and Most Reverend God that due an adequate provision be made, this day and the date hereinafter subscribed, for the satisfying of these petitioners' nutritional requirements, and for the organizing of such methods of allocation and distribution as may be deemed necessary and proper to assure the reception by and for said petitioners of such quantities of baked cereal products as shall, in the judgment of the aforesaid petitioners, constitute a sufficient supply thereof.

That only covers verse 11!

What makes this petition so hard is the three-letter word *and*. And ties the two verses together. What you are saying is "take care of my needs today and, at the same time, forgive my sins in the same way that I have forgiven those who have hurt me." Oh, how I wish the second part was not tied to the first!

Every time that I ask God to provide for my daily needs, I am to forgive those who have hurt me. Unfair.

Have you noticed that forgiveness is the only part of the prayer that Jesus emphasized and expanded? After finishing the Prayer, He immediately commented: "For if you forgive men when they sin against you, your heavenly Father will also forgive you. But if you do not forgive men their sins, your Father will not forgive your sins" (Matt. 6:14–15). Perhaps Jesus emphasized forgiveness because it is so easy to say but so difficult to give.

Could it be then that God's forgiveness is based on the way we forgive?

In the late fourth and fifth centuries, it was reported that churches were deleting this part of the prayer because they couldn't believe that God's forgiveness is conditional upon a forgiving spirit within the person seeking His pardon.

What makes forgiveness so hard is that we are called to forgive those who have hurt us—those who don't deserve it. There was a lady in my church who went out of her way to find fault in everything I did. She even went as far as telling lies about me. I even asked her what I did wrong and to forgive me. She responded with an emphatic "no." Then she said, "God has not told me to forgive you." She was the treasurer, and it got to the point that she progressed from taking the title *Reverend* off my paycheck to leaving my name off the paycheck completely and changing the date to make me wait to get paid. I got very angry and quit praying for her. From a human standpoint, I felt very justified, but slowly, God began to convict me, and I hated that. Then He said, "I forgave you when you didn't deserve it."

> "You have heard that it was said, 'You shall love your neighbor and hate your enemy.' But I say to you, love your enemies and pray for those who persecute you, so that you may be sons of your Father who is in heaven; for He causes His sun to rise on *the* evil and *the* good, and sends rain on *the* righteous and *the* unrighteous. (Matthew 5:43–45, NASB)

It took a power beyond me to forgive her. It took the power of the Holy Spirit. Slowly I began to pray, "Sick 'em, Lord." Then my prayer became more real, and I asked God to help me forgive. After two weeks, I was able to forgive her.

Greg Laurie: "Loving our enemies is certainly something that does not come easily—or naturally. In fact, if we wait for some feeling of love to suddenly overtake us, it simply won't happen. We must begin to pray for our enemies even before we are conscious of loving them. This is absolutely impossible to do apart from the help of the Holy Spirit."

I remind you of an old *Amos 'n' Andy* radio program. Andy became fed up with a big man who slapped him across the chest every time they met. "I'm ready for him," Andy tells Amos. "I put a stick of dynamite in my vest pocket, and the next time he slaps me, he's going to get his hand blown off." That makes us chuckle until we remember the dynamite of *hatred* may wound someone else while destroying us.

When we do not forgive someone who has harmed us, we allow bitterness to creep in. Bitterness is like a metastasized cancer. It contaminates every healthy thing it contacts. Charles Stanley wrote: "Holding on to hurt is like grabbing a rattlesnake by the tail; you are going to get bitten."

Bitterness cannot be contained. It always spreads. Forgiveness is the antidote to bitterness. It is not an option, any more than withholding the anti-venom from a snakebite victim is. Bitterness will destroy.

Every time that we pray, we must ask, who do I need to forgive?

Part 3: Help Me Run from Temptation

And lead us not into temptation. (Matt. 6:13)

One boy was heard praying, "And lead us not into Penn Station but deliver us from eagles." We, if we are honest, just jump over this line and don't really give it much thought. Lead us not into temptation...is that saying that God leads us into temptation? No. What it is, is Hebrew poetry. It is used to accent the next statement. "Deliver us from evil." It is like saying, "Give us not darkness, but give us light."

There are two kinds of evil in the world: moral evil and natural evil. The earthquake in Japan was a prime example of natural evil.

Prayer never guarantees that natural evil will bypass you.

However, in spite of natural evil, we can trust our Heavenly Father. Do you remember the story of Shadrach, Meshach, and Abednego? They were about to be thrown into the furnace when they said, "Our God will deliver us. Even if he chooses not to, we still will serve him." That same confidence will work with natural evil as well as with moral evil.

Man's rebellious spirit lies at the heart of moral evil. Moral evil is personal. It is a byproduct of God's love for us—in that he gave us free will and the right to choose good or bad.

> When tempted, no one should say, "God is tempting me." For God cannot be tempted by evil, nor does he tempt anyone; but each one is tempted when, by his own evil desire, he is dragged away and enticed. Then, after desire has conceived, it gives birth to sin; and sin, when it is full-grown, gives birth to death. (James 1:13–15)

The word *entice* (verse 14) is a fishing term. When you fish, you've got to provide bait that interests and entices a fish. I really like to fish for bass. My father-in-law taught me how to correctly use water dogs for bait. After learning to hook them properly, I was able to hook them and keep them alive. They would swim in the water, enticing the bass. The bass could not resist; if I handled things just right, I would get a sure strike. Then I would set the hook and enjoy my food

I don't know how fish think, but they probably think something like, "Wow, that looks great!" And when that fish leaves his hiding place for the bait, he's as good as caught.

As long as we remain obedient to the Lord, drawing our strength and our power from Him, the world around us can drop all sorts of bait and it won't seriously interest us. Oh, it's there. That is why we must pray daily, "Don't let me be tempted."

But when we choose to "forget" that God is in us and we slip out after the bait, we're hooked.

A friend of mine works at a casino. His job is to empty the slot machines. He then goes into a room and counts all the money. He handles thousands of coins a night. I asked him if he has ever been tempted to take a few dollars. He told me that he doesn't think of it as money.

A glance at your dictionary will inform you that temptation is "the act of enticement to do wrong, by promise of pleasure or gain." That's right! Temptation motivates you to be bad by promising something good. Isn't that just like the devil?

I heard a story about a very overweight man who went on a diet and lost a substantial amount of weight. His one weakness was sweets. He had changed his route to work so that he could avoid the bakery that was on his old way to work. One morning, he came to work carrying a large coffee cake.

He said, "This is a very special cake. I accidentally went the old way to work. As I approached the bakery, I prayed, 'Lord, if you want me to have one of those pastries, let me have the parking space next to the front door.'" And sure enough, the eighth time around the block, there was the empty space.

While we laugh at that illustration, I can't help but wonder, how many times do we go near the temptation that we are the weakest to handle? How many times do we think about it?

In Genesis 39 is the story of Joseph and Potiphar's wife. She is extremely beautiful, and it's just she and Joseph at home.

And Potiphar's wife has a lustful desire for Joseph and says, "Lie with me." She did this several times. Now, that's what I'd call dropping the bait! Nothing subtle about Mrs. Potiphar!

One day, she, looking very desirable, grabs him by the cloak. The cloak comes off. Instead of giving in to the strong temptation, he runs out of the house at full speed. He ran like mad.

Don't play with temptation. If you do, you will lose. Each day, I challenge you to pray, "Lead us not into temptation."

> No temptation has overtaken you but such as is common to man; and God is faithful, who will not allow you to be tempted beyond what you are able, but with the temptation will provide the way of escape also, so that you will be able to endure it. (1 Cor. 10:13)

Look for that way out and run for it.

Part 4: The Kingdom and the Power

For Thine is the kingdom, and the power, and the glory forever. Amen.

Our passage has an interesting history. It does not appear in *any* of the original manuscripts! It is both a prayer of submission and a doxology—a declaration of praise to God or a brief hymn expressing His power and glory. Several passages in the Bible are called doxologies because of their clear declaration of praise to God.[1]

The *Didache* (an early Christian teaching) lists this doxology—hymn—as being sung in the early church after the reading of Matthew 6:9–13. It was so commonly used that it eventually ended up in the Greek manuscripts.

With the addition of "for Thine...amen," the prayer now begins and ends in praise.

- Thine is the Kingdom = Jesus.
- The Power = the Holy Spirit
- The Glory = God the Father

When we conclude with the *kingdom*, *power*, and *glory*, we are submitting our wills to God's will for our lives. Earlier in

---

1   Ronald F. Youngblood, F. F. Bruce, R. K. Harrison, and Thomas Nelson Publishers, *Nelson's New Illustrated Bible Dictionary* (Nashville: Thomas Nelson, 1995).

the prayer, we were asking for His Kingdom to come; and at the end, we are acknowledging that His Kingdom is ruling over and in us.

Thy Kingdom come.

A simpleminded, illiterate man in England accepted Jesus as LORD and savior. He joined the local Salvation Army. His wife didn't know what was taking place, but she knew he was happy. One day he came back from the Salvation Army meeting unhappy.

"What's wrong?" she asked.

"They all have red sweaters," he answered, "and I don't have a red sweater." So she knitted him a red sweater. The first time he wore his red sweater, he came back from the Salvation Army sad again.

"What's wrong now?" his wife asked.

"They all have yellow writing on their red sweaters," he answered. The woman, who was illiterate also, promised to embroider some yellow writing on his red sweater. She crossed the street to a shop window, copied some letters, and embroidered them on his red sweater.

Off her husband went, wearing his red sweater with yellow writing. He was all smiles when he arrived home from visiting the Salvation Army.

"Did they like your sweater?" she asked.

"Yes."

"Did they like the writing?"

"Yes."

"What did they say?"

"They said they liked the writing on my sweater better than the writing on theirs."

She had unknowingly written across his chest, "This business is under new management."

By praying the doxology, we are admitting that we have a new manager—God.

The doxology says, "For Thine is…the power" (emphasis added). Devotional writer Mendell Taylor reminds us that "our Father" has "power enough to fling whirling worlds from His fingertips and to keep them moving with clocklike precision in their orbits. He has power to mix the colors of flowers and map the course of atoms. He has power to roll out carpets of green from coast to coast and tack them down with violets and daffodils." F. B. Meyer added, "He has the power to set up His kingdom, to overcome evil with good, hate with love, and darkness with light." God's power works for our good and His glory! And that power is at work in us.

In 1924, opera singer Roland Hayes stood to sing in a concert hall in Berlin. Many in his audience hated African Americans. Hayes described that night: "At eight o'clock, I walked onto the stage…a barrage of hisses, full of hatred, greeted me. I felt those hisses as if they were arrows aimed at my breast."

That great singer bowed his head and prayed, not that his talents would dazzle the audience, but that God's Spirit would flow through his songs. With hands folded and eyes closed, he prayed that God would sweep away racial hatreds. At last, the hisses died down. Silence.

Then Hayes sang the clear notes and message of Schubert's "Thou Art My Peace." When the last tones died away, the crowd responded with deafening applause. Hayes reported about that experience: "It was not a personal victory; it was the victory of God which sang through me. I was allowing myself to be used by a power...greater than I."

God's power remains available to us for every situation we encounter. We must plug into the power of the Holy Spirit. His is the kingdom, the power, and the glory.

For Thine is the kingdom, and the power, and the glory forever. Amen.

Part 5: I'm Finished, Lord!

The glory: Amen.

The glory—it's amazing, isn't it? That I can take a cucumber seed, not knowing if it is right side up or upside down, place it in some potting soil, add some water, and in sixty days, I have cucumbers. How does having cukes relate to God's glory? I look at the seed and plant and see the simplicity and complexity. And all I can say is, "For Thine is the glory." When we pray to our Father in heaven and realize that we can't be the only one praying at the same time and that he is attentively listening to all of us at the same time. All I can say is, "For Thine is the glory."

Amen.

Bible commentator Andrew Macleran wrote, "*Amen* is the expression of assured expectancy and confidence."

Randall Denny says, "*AMEN* IS NOT a closing punctuation or sign-off. It expresses confident trust that our all-wise Father has heard our prayers and that our all-powerful Father will do what is best for us; therefore we relax in faith."

In the Hebrew אמן, *amen*'s root meaning is "true, firm, solid, certain," and what it expresses is an emphatic yes to what has been said. "Definitely yes."

When we are saying *amen*, we are stating the fact that we believe the answer is coming. We are praying with trust in God.

> This is the confidence we have in approaching God: that if we ask anything according to his will, he hears us. And if we know that he hears us—whatever we ask—we know that we have what we asked of him. (1 John 5:14–15, NIV)

We should always pray with faith, believing God is going to answer. The amen should be a step of faith so powerful that we begin to act on it.

Luthi wrote about *amen*:

> Thanks to this abundant use of the Amen, the services were rather different from those we know today. The

congregation did not sit there silently as if they were not taking part. Any man who was not (teaching or preaching) could at any time join in with his Amen of faith when the Spirit moved him.

The preacher of today is in such a solitary position in his pulpit. Even though he knows that he is accompanied by many a silent Amen, how lonely he is when the community sends him into battle... Things were different in the communities of the New Testament. The Christians in Ephesus, Corinth, or Rome were not giving cheap applause; no, each one of them was taking an active part in the battle of the Spirit and the spirits with his contributory and supporting Amen. What a power of rejoicing when a crowd of believers confirms a prayer of thanks with their "Amen."

What a powerful word *amen* is. It is not a "hanging up the phone, I'm through" kind of ending. It is an "I commit my requests to you, God, and I know that you are going to answer my prayer according to your will" kind of ending. That's a prayer of faith, and that kind of praying is pleasing to God.

Be Well and Prosper?

Five times I received from the Jews the forty lashes minus one. Three times I was beaten with rods, once I was stoned, three times I was shipwrecked, and I spent a night and a day in the open sea, I have been constantly on the move. I have been in danger from rivers, in danger from bandits, in danger from my own countrymen, in danger from Gentiles; in danger in the city, in danger in the country, in danger at sea; and in danger from false brothers. I have labored and toiled and have often gone without sleep; I have known hunger and thirst and have often gone without food; I have been cold and naked. (2 Cor. 11:24–27, NIV)

Dear friends, do not be surprised at the painful trial you are suffering, as though something strange were happening to you. But rejoice that you participate in the sufferings of Christ, so that you may be overjoyed when his glory is revealed. (1 Pet. 4:12–13)

And at the ninth hour Jesus cried out in a loud voice, "Eloi, Eloi, lama sabachthani?"—which means, "My God, my God, why have you forsaken me?" (Mark 15:34)

HAVE YOU NOTICED that most of the TV preachers, lately, have been preaching that God wants to bless us and what is holding him back is our failure to verbalize our blessing? They also teach that if we want financial relief, we must send them money. I listen to the TV preachers tell me that God wants to bless me and prosper me, and I begin to wonder, *Why do I have Parkinson's—the disease that never lets you forget that you have it?*

One of the most famous of the blessed and prosper preachers is Joel Osteen. "Our message every single week is—through faith in God, you can live an overcoming life of victory....I believe that is the message this generation needs to hear. We've heard a lot about the judgment of God and what we can't do and what's going to keep us out of heaven. But it's time people start hearing about the goodness of God, about a God that loves them. A God that believes in them. A God that wants to help them. That's our message here at Lakewood."

"See, the Bible says that we can grow in favor," said Osteen in his sermon. "Increasing in favor," he says. "I believe one of the main ways that we grow in favor is by declaring it. It is not enough to just read it. It's not enough to just believe it. You've got to speak it out. Your words have creative power. And one of the primary ways we release our faith is through our words. And there is a divine connection between you declaring God's favor and you seeing God's favor manifest in your life…You've got to give life to your faith by speaking it out."

In his book, *Your Best Life Now*, Osteen tells how he and his wife got the house of their dreams by believing, seeing, and speaking that it could happen. "God has so much more in store for you too," Osteen says. "Start making room for it in your thinking. Start seeing yourself rising to a new level, doing something of significance, living in that house of your dreams."

God wants his children to prosper and enjoy good health. We need to claim the prosperity that is the birthright of every Christian.

He goes on to say, "The Bible says, 'God takes pleasure in prospering his children.' As his children prosper spiritually, physically, and materially, their increase brings pleasure to God. Your lot in life is to continually increase. Your lot in life is to be an overcomer, to live prosperously in every area."

As I said, I begin to wonder, *What is wrong with me? Do I still have Parkinson's because I have not declared my healing? Did Kathi—my wife—leave me because I did not declare my marriage as perfect? Am I not ahead financially because I lack the faith to believe that God wants to prosper me? Is God just waiting for me to change my thinking before He chooses to bless me?* The more I wonder, the more I am drawn to the Bible for answers.

Could it be that the apostle Paul, when suffering from the "thorn in his flesh," did not speak the proper words to be healed? Where were the blessings of God when Paul was beaten with rods, once was stoned, three times was shipwrecked, spent a night and a day in the open sea, "was constantly on the move. Was in danger from rivers, in danger from bandits, in danger from his own countrymen, in danger from Gentiles; in danger in the city, in danger in the country, in danger at sea; and in danger from false brothers. When he labored and toiled and went without sleep; when he was hungry and thirsty and went without food; was cold and naked"?

Or look at Jesus in the garden when the pressure to quit was almost too much for Him to bear.

> Then He said to them, "My soul is overwhelmed with sorrow to the point of death. Stay here and keep watch with me." (Matt. 26:38)

> And being in anguish, He prayed more earnestly, and His sweat was like drops of blood falling to the ground. (Luke 22:44, NIV)

Or when Jesus was on the cross, "My God, my God, why have you forsaken me?"

If He only spoke the right words, perhaps He might have been spared the agony of the cross.

All of us will face times when it seems that our prayers are getting nowhere and it seems like the storms of life are about to sink our ship. I do not really understand why we have to experience suffering. What I am *sure* of is that God does not cause our hardships—Satan does. (Why God allows them is something that I'll understand when I get to Heaven.) James, Philippians, and other books of the Bible speak of suffering. I am also convinced that speaking some special words will not help to end our suffering.

I am further convinced that we do not have to face our troubles alone. Let these words give you encouragement.

> If you love me, you will obey what I command. And I will ask the Father, and He will give you another Counselor to be with you forever—the Spirit of truth. The world cannot accept Him, because it neither sees Him nor knows Him. But you know Him, for he lives with you and will be in you. I will not leave you as orphans; I will come to you. (John 14:15–18)

> And so He does…He comes on those dark and stormy nights that we all face—He comes and offers us His comfort, and offers us His peace. (John 14:27, NIV)

> Peace I leave with you; my peace I give you. I do not give to you as the world gives. Do not let your hearts be troubled and do not be afraid. Come to me, all you who are weary and burdened, and I will give you rest. Take my yoke upon you and learn from me, for I am

gentle and humble in heart, and you will find rest for your souls. For my yoke is easy and my burden is light. (Matt. 11:28–30)

It is I; don't be afraid. (John 6:20)

Till the Storm Passes

In the dark of the midnight have I oft hid my face,
While the storm howls above me, and there's no hiding place.
'Mid the crash of the thunder, Precious Lord, hear my cry,
Keep me safe till the storm passes by.

Chorus

Till the storm passes over, till the thunder sounds no more,
Till the clouds roll forever from the sky;
Hold me fast, let me stand in the hollow of Thy hand, Keep me safe till the storm passes by.
Many times Satan whispered, "There is no need to try, for there's no end of sorrow, there's no hope by and by"
But I know Thou art with me, and tomorrow I'll rise where the storms never darken the skies.

Chorus

Till the storm passes over, till the thunder sounds no more,
Till the clouds roll forever from the sky;

Hold me fast, let me stand in the hollow of Thy hand, Keep me safe till the storm passes by.

When the long night has ended and the storms come no more,

Let me stand in Thy presence on the bright peaceful shore; In that land where the tempest, never comes, Lord, may I Dwell with Thee when the storm passes by.

Chorus

Till the storm passes over, till the thunder sounds no more,

Till the clouds roll forever from the sky;

Hold me fast, let me stand in the hollow of Thy hand, Keep me safe till the storm passes by.

The Tongue

When we put bits into the mouths of horses to make them obey us, we can turn the whole animal. Or take ships as an example. Although they are so large and are driven by strong winds, they are steered by a very small rudder wherever the pilot wants to go. Likewise the tongue is a small part of the body, but it makes great boasts. Consider what a great forest is set on fire by a small spark. The tongue also is a fire, a world of evil among the parts of the body. It corrupts the whole person, sets the whole course of his life on fire, and is itself set on fire by hell. All kinds of animals, birds, reptiles and creatures of the sea are being tamed and have been tamed by man, but no man can tame the tongue. It is a restless evil, full of deadly poison. With the tongue we praise our Lord and Father, and with it we curse men, who have been made in God's likeness. Out of the same mouth come praise and cursing. My brothers, this should not be. Can both fresh water and

> salt water flow from the same spring? My brothers, can
> a fig tree bear olives, or a grapevine bear figs? Neither
> can a salt spring produce fresh water. (James 3:3–12)

THE HOLY SPIRIT's presence has been felt in a very strong way this month. Several came to the altar during the altar call. The worship team has been right on, there is a spirit of excitement and anticipation that I have not felt in a long time. God is doing a great work in us. The pastor's sermon two weeks ago was heartfelt, and an excellent sermon was heard. With so much good, I almost dread writing what I am about to write. I remember the words of Smokey the Bear, who turned seventy this year: "Only you can prevent forest fires."

Think of this devotion as a means of fire protection.

It has been said that "a lie is halfway around the world while truth is still putting its shoes on." This illustrates the power of malicious speech. One unfounded rumor, one careless remark, one morsel of gossip can cause the greatest devastation. How correct James was when he wrote that the tongue is a flame of fire and full of wickedness.

Unfortunately, it is the sins of the tongue—backbiting, gossip, and tearing down another person—that we often excuse. James makes it clear that certain kinds of speech are wrong. After all, part of the fruit, or evidence of the Holy Spirit's presence in our lives is self-control (Gal. 5:22–23). The person who has no control over his or her tongue is usually "out of control" in other areas of life. But the person who has discipline over this area of life has yielded to the control of the Holy Spirit and will undoubtedly keep other areas of his or her life in check as well.

1. The tongue makes great boasts.

    "Likewise the tongue is a small part of the body, but it makes great boasts."

    Though it is a very small member of the body, the tongue can boast of great accomplishments, both good and evil. It can boast great things. It will cause us to brag about our ability, talents, possessions, spirituality, and accomplishments.

    > "Mirror, mirror on the wall, who's the fairest of them all? I am."
    >
    > "Count your blessings, name them one by one, and see what you have done."
    >
    > "When you're as great as I am, it is hard to be humble."
    >
    > —Muhammad Ali

2. The tongue is a fire.

    A cigarette butt, carelessly thrown, may start a brush fire. This in turn may ignite "a forest" and leave a charred mass of ruins. One of the great catastrophes of history was the Chicago fire of 1871. Tradition has it that it started when Mrs. O'Leary's cow kicked over her lantern. Whether or not that was true, the fire burned for three days over three and one half square miles of the city. It killed 250 people, made 100,000 homeless, and destroyed property valued at $175,000,000.

The Oakland Fire Department has determined that a five-alarm blaze that charred fifteen acres and threatened homes was accidentally caused by a spark from a Weed eater.

The tongue is like a small lighted match or a turned-over lantern. Its potentials for wickedness are almost infinite.

"Tillie told me that you told her that secret I told you not to tell her."

The other replied, "She's a mean thing. I told Tillie not to tell you I told her."

The first speaker responded, "Well, I told Tillie I wouldn't tell you she told me—so don't tell her I did."

The old verse "Sticks and stones will break my bones, but words will never hurt me" is a lie; words can and do destroy.

Think about the effect of your words on your marriage, on your employees, on our church, your children, on your family. Are you critical, easily angered, never satisfied, always negative?

3. The tongue is an untamed animal.

Nearly all animals may be domesticated. But the tongue is like a poisonous serpent. It will not subject itself to the human will.

> With the tongue we praise our Lord and Father, and with it we curse men, who have been made in God's likeness. Out of the same mouth come praise and cursing. My brothers, this should not be.

> We come to church on Sunday and use our tongue for its highest possible purpose…to sing praises to the Lord. Then we walk out, get into the car, and snap at those we love.

When the Scripture talks about *cursing*, it is not referring to just profanity—it means any kind of "put down." Even gossiping and constructive criticism; it was said of one person that he had a "very keen sense of rumor"!

Gossip is generally masked. It is easily rationalized.

> I heard it from a trusted source,
> so there's no cause to doubt it,
> and only tell it now, of course,
> so you can pray about it
> (Ken Anderson)

There are those Christians who feel that they must pray in a *loud* pious voice. "Now, God, please forgive Johnny for his adultery last night." That is nothing more than pious gossip.

Bruce Larson wrote, "How often we Christians have assumed that our job is to underscore other people's problems, sins, and mistakes! When we really believe in the Holy Spirit and the work which God has said He would do in every heart, then we know that our job is not to criticize. It is the Holy Spirit's job to convict. Not ours."

Someone said, "Christians are not meant to take the place of the Holy Spirit and become superdetectives, ferreting out people's sins and weaknesses and underscoring them. When we employ this kind of strategy, it is no wonder people fail to discover the grace of God in and through us."

When we get right down to the root of the problem, we find that it's not really a tongue problem—it is a heart problem.

> Don't you see that whatever enters the mouth goes into the stomach and then out of the body? But the things that come out of the mouth come from the heart, and these make a man "unclean." (Matt. 15:17–18, NIV)

In the sixth chapter of Isaiah, we see a scene in which Isaiah sees the Lord, high and exalted, and the train of his robe fills the temple.

> Above the throne of the Lord were 6 winged seraphs—angels who were calling to one another: Holy, holy, holy is the LORD Almighty; the whole earth is full of his glory. Isaiah says that the door posts and thresholds shook and the whole place was filled with smoke. As Isaiah stood there watching, he said "Woe to me! I am ruined! For I am a man of unclean lips, and I live among a people of unclean lips, and my eyes have seen the King, the LORD Almighty." As

soon as he finished speaking, one of the seraphs flew towards him with a hot coal in his hand. He placed the hot coal on Isaiah's lips and said, "See, this has touched your lips; your guilt is taken away and your sin atoned for." Then Isaiah heard the voice of the Lord saying, "Whom shall I send? And who will go for us?" And he said, "Here am I. Send me!"

What's the significance of the lips being purged?

By the seraph purging his lips, he was cleansing Isaiah's heart. After that, Isaiah was able to prophecy great things about the coming of Christ.

We too need our lips and hearts purged if we are going to do any good for Jesus. We are called to be imitators of God, and without the purging of our heart, that will be impossible. Our tongues will curse and bless. We will be like the board member who one Sunday morning stood up in church and gave a great testimony of how much he loved Jesus and, at the restaurant that afternoon, chewed the waitress up one side and down another. Nothing was right. He had her in tears.

We never know when our walk will be tested, and unless our hearts and tongues are purged by the Holy Spirit, we will say what we shouldn't say and do what we shouldn't do.

We must remember that our speech mirrors the condition of our heart. Our heart represents our innermost thoughts, desires, and emotions. If our heart is filled with bitterness, our speech will be tainted by it. If it is filled with the love of God, our words will also express that love.

Here is a good rule to apply before you speak: THINK.

> T—Is it *t*rue?
> H—Is it *h*elpful?
> I—Is it *i*nspiring?
> N—Is it *n*ecessary?
> K—Is it *k*ind?

> Don't say anything that would hurt [another person]. Instead, speak only what is good so that you can give help wherever it is needed. That way, what you say will help those who hear you. (Eph. 4:29, gw)

How is your speech? Are you always putting people down, always bragging about what you have, do you love to gossip? Are you critical, easily angered, never satisfied, or always negative?

You can't tame your tongue by yourself, but I know one who can; the Lord Jesus is willing and able to tame your tongue and clean your heart. Won't you let Him?

Rejoice

Rejoice in the Lord always. I will say it again: Rejoice! Let your gentleness be evident to all. The Lord is near. Do not be anxious about anything, but in everything, by prayer and petition, with thanksgiving, present your requests to God. And the peace of God, which transcends all understanding, will guard your hearts and your minds in Christ Jesus. Finally, brothers, whatever is true, whatever is noble, whatever is right, whatever is pure, whatever is lovely, whatever is admirable—if anything is excellent or praiseworthy— think about such things. (Phil. 4:4–8)

PAUL WAS WRITING from prison, where he was being held as a result of false accusations. Not only were the conditions bad, he was separated from those he loved, his motives had been questioned, and he had been misrepresented. He suffered physically and faced imminent execution.

I believe that it is in prison where Paul learned the keys to peace.

1.   He rejoiced in the Lord.

> Rejoice in the Lord always. I will say it again: Rejoice!
> Let your gentleness be evident to all. The Lord is near.

It is important to note that Paul does not say, "Rejoice in your situation or circumstance," he says to rejoice in the Lord.

Sometimes the trials and pressures of life make it almost impossible to be happy. But Paul did not tell us to be happy. He encourages us to rejoice in the Lord. In fact, he said it twice in verse 4.

Joy is the quiet, confident assurance of God's love and work in our lives—that he will be there no matter what! It is the reassurance that He will never leave us nor forsake us.

Happiness depends on happenings, but joy depends on our relationship with Christ.

Joy is one of the results of being filled with the Holy Spirit—the more the Spirit, the more the joy.

Could it be that a joyless Christian is an oxymoron?

Paul's attitude teaches us an important lesson: our inner attitudes do not have to reflect our outward circumstances. Paul was full of joy because he knew that no matter what happened to him, Jesus Christ was with him. Several times in this letter, Paul urges us to be joyful. It's easy to get discouraged about unpleasant circumstances. If you haven't been joyful lately, you may not be looking at life from the right perspective.

True joy comes from Christ dwelling within us. He will never fail us nor leave us, and in that we must rejoice!

> God is our refuge and strength, an ever-present help in trouble. (Ps. 46:1)

> I will not leave you as orphans; I will come to you. (John 14:18)

No matter what goes on in this life, no matter how rough it gets, you can still rejoice in the Lord!

2. He trusted Jesus with everything.

> Do not be anxious about anything, but in everything, by prayer and petition, with thanksgiving, present your requests to God. (Phil. 4:6)

The idea is that the believer is not to worry or fret about a single thing. The word *nothing* means "not even one thing." Humanly speaking, the Philippians had every reason to worry and be anxious. In the midst of such circumstances, the only way a person can keep from worrying is to receive an injection of supernatural power.

This is the very point of Scripture. There is an answer to worry and anxiety, a supernatural answer: the peace of God. God will enable the believer to conquer worry and anxiety. God will infuse the believer with peace—with the very peace of God Himself—a peace so great and so wonderful that it carries the believer right through the trial.

The remedy for anxiety and worry is prayer.

> Do not be anxious about anything, but in everything, by prayer and petition, with thanksgiving, present your requests to God. And the peace of God, which transcends all understanding, will guard your hearts and your minds in Christ Jesus. (Phil. 4:6–7)

If we will learn to pray more and worry less, there will come upon us a wonderful peace—the peace that surpasses all understanding.

> It is beyond anything we can ask or think. It surpasses all our imaginations. Think of the most terrible situation you can imagine; then think of the peace you would want as you went through that trial. In actual experience, the peace of God is far greater than anything you could ever imagine or understand. The peace of God actually carries the faithful believer through the very midst of trial and tribulation.
>
> But also note that this is a guarding peace. This peace of God that is offered will "guard your hearts

and minds in Christ Jesus." The peace of God is like a most elite soldier who guards and protects the most precious possession of God: the believer's heart and mind.

We can know the peace of God only if we have trusted Christ as our Lord and Savior and only if we walk in fellowship with Him. To be in Christ means to walk in Christ—to live, move, and have our being in Him.

This peace is offered to each of us if we will make our needs known to Him and trust Him with them.

3. He found good things to focus his attention on.

    Finally, brothers, whatever is true, whatever is noble, whatever is right, whatever is pure, whatever is lovely, whatever is admirable—if anything is excellent or praiseworthy—think about such things. (Phil. 4:8)

    Paul tells us to program our minds with thoughts that are true, noble, right, pure, lovely, admirable, excellent, and praiseworthy. Whatever we are facing, we must try to find one thing to praise the Lord about. Once our minds get trained in this manner, it will be easier to do.

    We must turn our eyes upon Jesus and not our struggles. We must look to not what is temporary but what is eternal.

4. The Lord became the source of his strength.

> I can do everything through him who gives me strength. (Phil. 4:13)

He could do all things through Christ. <u>Too many of us forget that. "God helps those who help themselves." Not!</u> so Paul realized that he could do anything and endure anything because of the power given to him by Christ. Without Christ taking charge of his life, he had no power or strength. In our weaknesses, we must allow Christ to give us strength.

What are you facing? What burden are you carrying? Turn to him and receive his peace.

> Peace I leave with you; my peace I give you. I do not give to you as the world gives. Do not let your hearts be troubled and do not be afraid. (John 14:27, NIV)

Only God Could Pull It Off
The Greatest Miracle

HERSHEL, THE JEW, upon really listening to the Christmas story for the first time, replied, "Oye, such a story. A virgin giving boyth to a baby? Let my daughter try that. *Cholileh* [Perish the thought], I am telling you, such a story. *Es iz nit geshtoigen un nit gefloigen!* [It never happened, it doesn't make sense]."

"Ven, the pope, was coming to town. The advance men came first."

"I know, I vas on that committee," he replied, puffing out his chest. "Ve had to remove the mail depositories from the parade route, arrange for a special security detail, and make preparations for the arrival of Shepherd One and the pope mobile. Ve spent weeks getting ready. Oye veyh, so much vork for such a visit."

"Are you telling me that supposedly God's son had no front men, no security force, and he wasn't offered the Lincoln bedroom to sleep in?"

"The messiah was born in a stable."

"*Cholileh!* Oye, it stinks in a stable. You're telling me your God, the messiah, was born in a stable?"

Hershel finally pauses, and the storyteller responds, "Hershel, don't say another word—let me explain. You see, it says in the New Testament in the book of John, 'In the beginning was the Word, and the Word was with God, and the Word was God. The Word became flesh and made his dwelling among us.' We have seen his glory, the glory of the One and Only, who came from the Father, full of grace and truth." A literal interpretation of the Greek states, "God pitched a tent and made His dwelling among the people."

For centuries, God kept telling us to stop sinning and to turn back to him. For centuries, God sought to restore His broken relationship with us due to our sinning. His love for us demanded it—His grace allowed it. He sent prophets, priests, and kings to warn us to change our ways and to remind us that He wanted a people He could call His own. We rejected His approaches—the gap, the division between God and our sinfulness, was just too great.

God's law was given to us through Moses. We did all we could to break it.

The law required judgment and punishment. "For the wages of sin is death—love and grace required mercy—the gift of God is eternal life in Christ Jesus our Lord" (Rom. 6:23).

The law said that blood must be shed in order to pay the penalty for our sins. The ancients sacrificed animals in the temple for forgiveness of our sins in accordance to the law. It proved futile as we kept on sinning.

> But when the proper time had fully come, God sent His Son, born of a woman, born subject to [the regulations of] the Law, To purchase the freedom of (to ransom, to redeem, to atone for) those who were subject to the Law, that we might be adopted and have sonship conferred upon us [and be recognized as God's sons]. (Gal. 4:4–5, AMP)

> For God so loved the world that he gave his one and only Son, that whoever believes in him shall not perish but have eternal life. For God did not send his Son into the world to condemn the world, but to save the world through him. (John 3:16–17)

In those words, we find our hope—God loves us and gave to us His Son.

> God made him who had no sin to be sin for us, so that in him we might become the righteousness of God. (2 Cor. 5:21)

The miracle of Christmas is that, at a point of time in human history, God put skin on His face. And it was the face of Jesus! A face full of love. By stepping into the stream of human history, by putting on flesh of our flesh, skin of our skin, and bone of our bones in Jesus of Nazareth, God was able to better communicate with us. By stepping into history, he was able to experience firsthand all that we experience.

> For we do not have a high priest who is unable to sympathize with our weaknesses, but we have one who has been tempted in every way, just as we are— yet was without sin. (Heb. 4:15, NIV)

It was one thing for God to become flesh. It was quite another thing for people to feel comfortable with divinity dwelling among them. Most of us would find it difficult to feel at ease if the president of the United States were our dinner guest. How much more difficult would it be for us—weak and fallible as we are—to feel comfortable in the presence of the sinless Son of God, the King of Kings, and the Lord of Lords!

How did God bridge the awesome social gap between God and man?

1. God allowed His Son to enter the world as a tiny, fragile, and very vulnerable baby.

    > It's amazing to me to watch the impact that babies have on people. Have you ever noticed that? Sure you have. I mean the presence of a baby does amazing things to adults. Take a group of normally sober-

minded adults, put them in a room and introduce into that setting a gurgling, bright-eyed baby and watch what happens. The whole countenance of the people changes. The eyes light up, the posture raises noticeably, the hands come together in "patty-cake" position, and the corners of the mouth turn up in the goofiest grin you've ever seen.

The miracle of the incarnation: God took the world by surprise by coming to us as a baby. Why? So that no one would feel intimidated in His presence.

2. Jesus was born into a blue-collar family. His dad was a carpenter. No royalty was found in his family. No aristocrats. Just common people.
3. Jesus was not born the son of a prophet or of a priest. He was never a member of the religious establishment of His time. Look at His descendants.

The Genealogy of Jesus

A record of the genealogy of Jesus Christ the son of David, the son of Abraham: Abraham was the father of Isaac, Isaac the father of Jacob, Jacob the father of Judah and his brothers, Judah the father of Perez and Zerah, whose mother was Tamar, Perez the father of Hezron, Hezron the father of Ram, Ram the father of Amminadab, Amminadab the father of Nahshon, Nahshon the father of Salmon, Salmon the father of

Boaz, whose mother was Rahab, Boaz the father of Obed, whose mother was Ruth, Obed the father of Jesse, and Jesse the father of King David. David was the father of Solomon, whose mother had been Uriah's wife, Solomon the father of Rehoboam, Rehoboam the father of Abijah, Abijah the father of Asa, Asa the father of Jehoshaphat, Jehoshaphat the father of Jehoram, Jehoram the father of Uzziah, Uzziah the father of Jotham, Jotham the father of Ahaz, Ahaz the father of Hezekiah, Hezekiah the father of Manasseh, Manasseh the father of Amon, Amon the father of Josiah, and Josiah the father of Jeconiah and his brothers at the time of the exile to Babylon. After the exile to Babylon: Jeconiah was the father of Shealtiel, Shealtiel the father of Zerubbabel, Zerubbabel the father of Abiud, Abiud the father of Eliakim, Eliakim the father of Azor, Azor the father of Zadok, Zadok the father of Akim, Akim the father of Eliud, Eliud the father of Eleazar, Eleazar the father of Matthan, Matthan the father of Jacob, and Jacob the father of Joseph, the husband of Mary, of whom was born Jesus, who is called Christ. (Matt. 1:1–16)

Tamar, Rahab. Solomon's mother, Bathsheba. You wouldn't think of these women (as well as most of the men) as the proper descendants of God. Tamar tricked her father-in-law Judah, Jacob's son, into having sex with her and gave birth to twins. Rahab was a prostitute. Bathsheba committed adultery. Ruth wasn't a Jew.

Manasseh was the wickedest king in all of history. Uzziah was struck with leprosy for performing the duties of a priest. Ahaz sacrificed his children to the god molech and stole from the temple. "He offered sacrifices and burned incense at the high places, on the hilltops, and under every spreading tree." Amon was so bad that his people turned against him. Why would the Son of God, the Savior of the universe, come from such questionable people? To show us that anyone can come to Him no matter our past or background.

4. Jesus took upon himself the form of a servant.

    > Just as the Son of Man did not come to be served,
    > but to serve, and to give his life as a ransom for many.
    > (Matt. 20:28)

5. He assumed the lowliest of social roles so that the humblest and most disadvantaged would not feel awkward and ill at ease in His presence.

    The Gospels tell us that the common people heard Jesus gladly.

6. Jesus knew suffering, abuse, rejection: "He came unto his own, and his own received him not" (John 1:11).

    He was misunderstood, mocked, and mobbed. He was poor, homeless, and owned no property apart from a seamless peasant's cloak. He was arrested, falsely accused, convicted, and condemned in a travesty of justice. He died a horrible death, executed as a common criminal so that every social outcast, every sinner—no matter how bad the sin—and those alone and abandoned could find a point of identity in Him.

Hershel let me sum it up with this story. In the early 1950s, a missionary to Africa contracted a disease in the African bush. The missionary was returned to the States to be treated for his illness. The doctors struggled and worked to bring about a cure, but were unsuccessful.

In just a few years, the missionary passed away, leaving his wife and three little boys. For several years, she tried to care for the boys alone. She was a nurse by trade and kept very difficult hours. But somehow, by the grace of God, she was able to keep her family together and put food on the table. God sent a wonderful Christian man into her life, and they were married, which also meant that those three boys had a new father.

His home was on the Oregon Coast, where it rained a lot—much different than what the family was accustomed to. And yet they gathered up their family, moved them across state lines, and moved in together.

The three boys were not impressed! They weren't sure about this new dad! They didn't want anything to do with him.

They decided to stand back and make him buy every inch of their affection and love. They were rude, they were cruel, they were undisciplined, and they were angry!

It all came to a head about Christmastime—the time when there are so many feelings and memories. And so the father packed up his saw and axe, piled those three boys in the back of his pickup truck, and headed up into the mountains to find a Christmas tree.

As they searched through the woods that day, slowly, but surely, they began to laugh and unwind. They were beginning to have a little fun when they came upon the perfect tree! Everybody voted that it was the one to have. Each one took a turn on the saw, and down it came!

They dragged it back to the pickup, threw it into the bed, and started home. But on the way, their Christmas tree did what all do in the trip home—it grew! When they put it in the stand, the problem was obvious. It was so tall that it scraped the top of the ceiling and bent over against the edge of the molding. There was a collective gasp! *What's Dad going to do about our Christmas tree?*

The father paused a moment, and then he drug out his toolbox, went up to the bedroom above the living room, and cut a hole in the ceiling! He cut through the carpet, through the boards, through the dry wall, everything!

It just happened to be the boys' bedroom. He placed the tree so that it poked through that hole, and they loved it. They had a tree upstairs and downstairs. They were absolutely ecstatic! In that moment, he became a father to them.

Through a simple action motivated by love, he said, "I will do anything to be a father to you!" That's what God is saying to you, Hershel, "I will do anything to be a father to you!"

Jesus felt our feelings. He knew our pain. A holy, infinite, all-knowing, all-powerful, creator, God cut a hole in the ceiling of heaven and let himself through!

He knows that we would struggle forever with "who He is" and "what He's like." He is aware that we need a God with "skin on His face."

He became the With-Us-God. Emmanuel. In the life, death, and resurrection of Jesus of Nazareth, we have seen God with skin on His face. And in Jesus, we have known the Father! That's why Jesus said, "If you have seen me, you have seen the Father." Jesus *is* God with us! Not God above us! Not God around us! Not God against us! But God *for* us!

For once in his life, Hershel was speechless.

What's So Amazing about Grace?

I WAS DRAWN to the book of Hosea recently. What an interesting story. God tells the prophet Hosea to marry a loose woman—a ho, as the expression goes, one who would commit adultery.

Hosea obeys the Lord and marries Gomer. And as expected, she commits adultery. He forgives her. She's pregnant and gives birth to a boy. Hosea suspects that the boy is not his.

Next she conceives and has a girl. Again, the product of adultery. Again, he forgives her. And again she cheats on him, and again she gets pregnant. Three children. None his. Each time, he shows her his love and forgiveness. He treats the kids as if they are his own, and treats her as if she had never cheated.

Gomer settles down for a while and becomes a pretty good wife, but she kept thinking about the past, the life without the children, without the responsibilities of a wife. It became too much, and she left. Hosea and the kids were heartbroken. They all missed her.

Hosea waited for her to return as she had before. After what seemed like a very long time, he heard the Lord tell him that it was time to find Gomer. He began the long walk to the red-light district. Unsure of where to look for her, he went to the slave market. Gomer was the next in line to be bid for. Hosea bargained with the owner. "So I bought her to me for fifteen pieces of silver, and for an homer of barley, and1 an half homer of barley" (3:2). As the prophet stepped forward to take his purchase, the once beautiful young woman hung her head in shame. She had sold herself as a slave to sin, and now she found herself helpless in literal slavery. But her husband was redeeming her.

As I said before, what a wonderful example of love. Can you grasp it? She cheated on him not once, but numerous times. Each time, Hosea forgave her, took her back, and trusted her.

There is more to the story; not only is it a great love story, it is a story of God's love and grace for us.

> But God demonstrates his own love for us in this: While we were still sinners, Christ died for us. (Rom. 5:8) For it is by grace you have been saved, through faith—and this not from yourselves, it is the gift of

God—not by works, so that no one can boast. (Eph. 2:8}

For the law was given through Moses; grace and truth came through Jesus Christ. (John 1:17)

What is this thing called grace?

The *Beacon Dictionary of Theology* defines it as "God's spontaneous, though unmerited, love for sinful man, supremely revealed in the life, death, and resurrection of Jesus Christ. Grace is a foundational element of the Gospel....grace excludes every pretense of merit on the part of the recipient. Grace is God's free, unmerited, and non-legal way of dealing with sinful man...the life; suffering, death, and resurrection of Jesus reflect the action of God's grace in history. (Taylor, Richard S.)

Someone else defined it as *God's riches at Christ's expense.* Grace cannot be earned, be repaid, nor is it deserved.

Grace says that anyone may ask for God's forgiveness. No matter the sin, how evil it may seem—it will be forgiven if you ask for God's forgiveness. Not only will it be forgiven, it will be forgotten. Can you grasp what that means?

Jeffrey Dahmer and Ted Bundy, two of the most evil men in all of history, have confessed their sins and received Jesus Christ as Savior. By doing that, they are both in heaven. It doesn't seem fair—those horrible men in heaven.

If you earnestly confess your sins, the slate is wiped clean. Your sin is forgotten and forgiven, just as if you had never sinned in the first place. It's called justification (just as if you did not sin). It is because of His amazing, amazing grace.

> But where sin increased, grace increased all the more. (Rom. 5:21)

Maybe you have never asked God to forgive you; you have never asked Jesus into your heart. You can do it right now—just as you are, deep in sin or not.

> That if you confess with your mouth, "Jesus is Lord," and believe in your heart that God raised him from the dead, you will be saved. For it is with your heart that you believe and are justified, and it is with your mouth that you confess and are saved. As the Scripture says, "Anyone who trusts in him will never be put to shame." You believe in your heart that God raised Jesus from the dead and you confess with your mouth that Jesus is Lord. That's it. It seems too easy. (Rom. 10:9–11, NIV)

A prayer: Jesus, please forgive me. I believe you rose from the dead and are alive today, come into my heart. I believe that you are Lord.

Then tell someone that "You belong to Christ. That's it. Now you belong to Jesus."

Politically Correct Sin

CAN YOU REMEMBER when it was okay to use the adjective *short* when referring to someone who was? Or calling someone blind, or deaf, handicapped? Or when someone who lacked hair on his head was called bald?

Can you remember when someone stole large sums of money from a corporation and was called an embezzler? Or when someone who was held in high esteem by society committed murder, how it seemed like the court was harder on him? Can you remember when a spouse committed adultery, and we called it adultery?

Times change and, I guess, so must our vocabulary. There needed to be a term for our changing vocabulary, and so the men of greatness formed the words *political correctness*:

> Political correctness (adjectivally, politically correct; both forms commonly abbreviated to PC) is a term applied to language, ideas, policies, or behavior seen

by some as seeking to minimize offense to gender, racial, cultural, disabled, aged or other identity groups. Conversely, the term "politically incorrect" is used to refer to language or ideas that may cause offense or that are unconstrained by orthodoxy. For example, the term "concentration camp," to describe camps used to confine civilian members of the Boer community in close (concentrated) quarters, was used by the British during the Second Boer War, primarily because it sounded bland and inoffensive. Despite the high death rates in the British concentration camps, the term remained acceptable as a euphemism. However, after the Third Reich used the expression to describe its death camps, the term gained enormous negative connotation. (Political Correctness)

The more PC we got, the more things changed:

Shell shock (World War I) → battle fatigue (World War II) → operational exhaustion (Korean War) → posttraumatic stress disorder (Vietnam War)

- *sanitary landfill* for *garbage dump* (and a temporary garbage dump is a *transfer station*), also often called a *Civic Amenity* in the UK
- *pre-owned vehicles* for *used cars*
- a student being *held back* a grade level for having *failed* or *flunked* the grade level
- *correctional facility* for *prison*

- *bathroom tissue*, *t.p.*, or *bath tissue* for *toilet paper* (usually used by toilet paper manufacturers)
- *custodian* for *janitor*
- *economically depressed neighborhood* or *culturally-deprived environment* for *ghetto*
- *force*, *police action*, or *conflict* for *war*
- *enhanced interrogation technique* for *torture*
- *gaming* for *gambling*
- *specific about what one eats* for being a *picky eater*
- *aggregate relocation specialist* for *dump truck driver*
- *intellectually challenged* or *special needs* for being *mentally retarded*
- *reduction in force* for *to lay off*
- *gender reassignment* for *sex change*
- *Montezuma's revenge* for *dysentery*
- *Passed away* for *died*
- *Privy* or *john* or *rest room* for *bathrooms*

Did you notice how by changing the *words* the terminology seems watered down? The situation or event doesn't sound so bad.

So now we have politically correct terms for *sin*:

- adulterers—swingers
- adultery—extramarital affair
- embezzlement—white-collar crime
- pro-abortion—reproductive rights, pro choice

- looters—undocumented shoppers
- losing control—road rage
- white lie—lie
- creative accounting—false set of books
- coveting—keeping up with the Joneses
- drunk—under the influence
- pornography—adult entertainment

Sin no longer seems dirty. Society excuses it by changing the terms. Political correctness is the norm. The problem is, according to God, sin is still sin. No matter what you call it. Politically correct or not.

> For the wages of sin is death, but the gift of God is eternal life in Christ Jesus our Lord. (Rom. 6:23, NIV)

A Messiah? A King?

As they approached Jerusalem and came to Bethphage on the Mount of Olives, Jesus sent two disciples, saying to them, "Go to the village ahead of you, and at once you will find a donkey tied there, with her colt by her. Untie them and bring them to me. If anyone says anything to you, tell him that the Lord needs them, and he will send them right away." This took place to fulfill what was spoken through the prophet: "Say to the Daughter of Zion, 'See, your king comes to you, gentle and riding on a donkey, on a colt, the foal of a donkey.'" The disciples went and did as Jesus had instructed them. They brought the donkey and the colt, placed their cloaks on them, and Jesus sat on them. A very large crowd spread their cloaks on the road, while others cut branches from the trees and spread them on the road. The crowds that went ahead of him and those that followed shouted, "Hosanna to the Son of David!" "Blessed is he who comes in the name of the Lord!" "Hosanna in the highest!" When Jesus entered Jerusalem, the whole city was stirred and asked, "Who is this?" (Matt. 21:1–10, NIV)

LET'S LOOK AT this through the eyes of someone who was there. Follow along with me as we imagine what it would have been like to witness this epic moment in history.

I was there that day. You see, I am a member of the temple police—part of the Sanhedrin. It's a good job with a lot of prestige and power. I am the one who will visit you if you miss the Sabbath services for a few weeks. I am also the one who is charged with enforcing temple law. I can make your life miserable if you break the law.

I too asked many times the same question of the crowd— who is this man Jesus?

He claimed to be a king and the messiah. A messiah? A king? Yeah right!

I remember doing a background check on him. He was born in a manger. Not a palace. What kind of messiah-king comes as a baby? I checked into the circumstances behind his birth and found out that Joseph didn't claim to be his real dad. Mary claims that she got pregnant by the Holy Spirit. Sure!

The visitors after he was born were some shepherds. What kind of king allows shepherds to visit him? They are the scum of the earth, and they aren't even allowed to be witnesses in a trial or serve on a jury.

That was it: no fanfare, no celebration, and no newspeople, no paparazzi —what kind of a king could this be? The messiah as a baby? God as a baby? The baby looked like anything but a king. His cry, though strong and healthy, was still the helpless and piercing cry of a baby. And he was absolutely dependent upon Mary for his well-being. Majesty in the midst of the mundane. Holiness in the filth of sheep manure and sweat. Divinity entering the world on the floor of a stable, through the womb of a teenager, and in the presence of a carpenter. Who is this baby Jesus? A messiah?

A king?

I watched as he was growing up. He astonished the teachers of the law in the temple when he was twelve. Where did he get his knowledge? He taught with authority, and somehow most of what he said made sense, unlike the scribes and the Pharisees.

I was at the wedding in Cana and watched as he saved the day. They had run out of wine before the party was over. This would cause embarrassment to the family. I listened as his mother told him to do something. I thought to myself, *What's he supposed to do?*

> Nearby stood six stone water jars, the kind used by the Jews for ceremonial washing, each holding from twenty to thirty gallons. Jesus said to the servants, "Fill the jars with water"; so they filled them to the brim. Then he told them, "Now draw some out and take it to the master of the banquet." They did so, and

the master of the banquet tasted the water that had been turned into wine. He did not realize where it had come from, though the servants who had drawn the water knew. Then he called the bridegroom aside and said, "Everyone brings out the choice wine first and then the cheaper wine after the guests have had too much to drink; but you have saved the best till now." This, the first of his miraculous signs, Jesus performed at Cana in Galilee. He thus revealed his glory, and his disciples put their faith in him. (John 2:6–11, NIV)

The disciples put their faith in him, but I didn't. It might have been some kind of magic trick.

I observed the people coming to him for healing. I remember one day in particular. The house in which Jesus was speaking was quite crowded, and these two guys were carrying their friend, hoping that Jesus would heal him. They could not even get to the door, so they did a strange thing: they carried him to the roof of the building, removed some of the roofing material, and lowered him through the hole that they had made. They worked together as a team in order to lower him into the house with ropes. I held my breath thinking that they were going to drop him.

When Jesus saw their faith, he said to the paralytic, "Son, your sins are forgiven." Now some teachers of the law were sitting there, thinking to themselves, "Why does this fellow talk like that? He's blaspheming! Who can forgive sins but God alone?" Immediately

> Jesus knew in his spirit that this was what they were
> thinking in their hearts, and he said to them, "Why
> are you thinking these things? Which is easier: to say
> to the paralytic, 'Your sins are forgiven,' or to say, 'Get
> up, take your mat and walk'? But that you may know
> that the Son of Man has authority on earth to forgive
> sins...." He said to the paralytic, "I tell you, get up,
> take your mat and go home." He got up, took his mat
> and walked out in full view of them all. This amazed
> everyone and they praised God, saying, "We have
> never seen anything like this!" (Mark 2:5–12, NIV)

Neither had I. Was this man really the messiah: could he
really be a king? A messiah? A king?

His actions puzzled me. He did not seem to respect the
Sabbath. He would heal on the day of rest—that was wrong,
or was it? He said something about an ox in a ditch. This
angered my bosses. I remember one day that a man with a
withered hand had come to the synagogue on the Sabbath.

> Jesus said to the man with the shriveled hand, "Stand
> up in front of everyone." Then Jesus asked them,
> "Which is lawful on the Sabbath: to do good or to
> do evil, to save life or to kill?" But they remained
> silent. He looked around at them in anger and, deeply
> distressed at their stubborn hearts, said to the man,
> "Stretch out your hand." He stretched it out, and his
> hand was completely restored. Then the Pharisees
> went out and began to plot with the Herodians how

> they might kill Jesus. Jesus withdrew with his disciples
> to the lake, and a large crowd from Galilee followed.
> (Mark 3:3–7, NIV)

They wanted to kill this man Jesus. I did not really see what he did that was so bad.

After all, the guy was healed. He did, in a way, make fun of their orthodoxy.

Then I watched as Jesus picked his team. What a strange bunch. Fishermen, a tax collector, a zealot, and a thief. Twelve men who had no leadership skills, no charisma.

Some of them were known for their violent tempers.

A messiah? A king?

There was a time when even his own family thought that he was crazy. After listening to some of his teachings, I began to wonder myself. He said some things like "in order to save one's life, you have to lose it," "for whatever is hidden is meant to be disclosed, and whatever is concealed is meant to be brought out into the open," "the first will be last and the last first." He talked about eating his flesh and drinking his blood.

He preached to turn the other cheek and even attacked the customs of the scribes and Pharisees. He told them to quit looking so pathetic when they fast, to pray quietly, and to give their tithes secretly. They did not like the way he attacked their "Godly" walk.

Then there was the day that he called himself I Am. And the day that he said that the Father and he were one. They were mad. They were secretly plotting to kill him.

Then there was the Sunday that he came into Jerusalem riding on a donkey. A king riding on a donkey—how absurd. The people began shouting "hosanna, hosanna, hosanna." I admit I was caught up in the excitement of the moment and began to utter a hosanna also. Then I got to think about the event; there was no entourage, there was no great announcement, no advance man to set up his visit, just this man Jesus coming into town riding on a donkey. I noticed tears in his eyes as he overlooked the city. Tears of joy, or tears of sadness? What kind of king rides a donkey anyway? A messiah? A king?

His next move astounded me. He went into the part of the temple called the court of the gentiles and observed for a moment the chaos that was there. There was Yitzhak selling his doves for the sacrifice: "Hey, you can have these for two zuzim." There was Mordecai offering his doves, three for two zuzim, slightly blemished. Over in the corner was the high priest presiding at the exchange table, exchanging the money of the people for the temple shekel. Jesus watched as the rate of exchange kept changing. If you appeared wealthy, your rate was set higher than the others; there was the customary arguing about this. In another corner stood Shlomo and his brothers taking bids for the doves. A regular auction, no less. The noise of the place was deafening. The next day, Jesus returned to the temple.

> On reaching Jerusalem, Jesus entered the temple area
> and began driving out those who were buying and

> selling there. He overturned the tables of the money
> changers and the benches of those selling doves, and
> would not allow anyone to carry merchandise through
> the temple courts. And as he taught them, he said,
> "Is it not written: 'My house will be called a house of
> prayer for all nations'? But you have made it 'a den of
> robbers.'" (Mark 11:15–17, NIV)

Wow! What nerve calling it his house. Boy, were the sellers
mad. He had put them out of business. That was it—they had
had it, he must go. The messiah? A king?

> Then Satan entered Judas, called Iscariot, one of the
> Twelve. And Judas went to the chief priests and the
> officers of the temple guard and discussed with them
> how he might betray Jesus. They were delighted and
> agreed to give him money. He consented, and watched
> for an opportunity to hand Jesus over to them when
> no crowd was present. (Luke 22:3–6, NIV)

I was on duty that day and remember the payment that
Judas received: thirty pieces of silver—the price of a slave.

I received the arrest warrant and accompanied the crowd
of soldiers; we were carrying swords and torches and other
weapons. What you would call today a SWAT team.

I thought, *How strange, a whole lot of people to capture one
unarmed man.* I watched as Judas approached Jesus and gave
him a kiss.

We took Jesus into custody and brought him before Annas, the ex–high priest, where he was questioned and then brought to Annas's son, Caiphus, the current high priest. I listened intently to the trial and noticed that no one's testimony against him agreed. *Wow,* I thought, *this is not good. He must be tried on the basis of two witnesses.* Then he was asked if he was the Christ, the Son of God. He replied simply, "I am." They declared his statement blasphemy and found him guilty. His sentence: death.

I then watched as he was slapped in the face and spit upon. This was no way to treat a prisoner. I wanted to help him, but I needed my job. As we had no power to put anyone to death, we then brought the prisoner to Pontius Pilate, the governor; he could carry out the sentence.

We left Jesus in the custody of the Romans and waited outside. Pilate appeared before the crowd a short time later and told the people that he found nothing wrong with Jesus. However, he offered to have him scourged in the hopes of pleasing the crowd. He then reminded them of the custom whereby a prisoner can be set free. The crowd shouted that they want Barabbas set free.

Pilate then asked, "What should I do with Jesus?" The crowd shouted, "Crucify him, crucify him." Pilate argued with the crowd, but their shouts prevailed. Jesus was then flogged, a crown of thorns was banged on his head, a staff was placed in his right hand, and was spit in his face, then they bowed in front of him and mocked him. They then took his staff and struck him on the head several times, the crown of thorns digging deeply into his scalp.

I flashed my badge and pushed my way through the crowd to take a closer look at Jesus. There he was standing before the crowd, his face wracked with pain, blood dripping down his face on to the ground from his scalp wounds. A messiah? A king?

I watched as he was nailed to the cross, and then the cross was lifted into place. The people were shouting insults at him.

Then I heard him speak words that I'll never forget: "Father, forgive them for they do not know what they are doing." A messiah? A king? Maybe.

A short time later, he died.

I was off Sunday and went for a stroll in the morning. I walked by the tomb after the earthquake struck. The giant stone that formed the door to the tomb was rolled back. I peeked inside and saw that it was empty. I remember hearing Jesus's followers say something about him rising from the dead. As I was thinking about this, I heard someone coming, so I hid in the bushes. What I saw was so amazing that I thought I was dreaming. There was Jesus talking to one of his followers—a woman. I blinked my eyes to make sure that what I was seeing was what I thought I saw. It was him.

He was alive. A messiah? A king? No, a savior. My savior. My messiah. My king.

Carrying Our Cross

Part 1: Trust

Then he said to them all: "If anyone would come after me, he must deny himself and take up his cross daily and follow me. For whoever wants to save his life will lose it, but whoever loses his life for me will save it. What good is it for a man to gain the whole world, and yet lose or forfeit his very self? (Luke 9:23–25)

TO CARRY ONE'S cross begins with complete trust in the Lord.

Trust in the LORD with all your heart and lean not on your own understanding; in all your ways acknowledge him, and he will make your paths straight. (Prov. 3:5–6, NIV)

If we are going to carry our cross, we must trust the one who it *really* belongs to.

Earl Lee wrote, "Trusting is to lean hard on the Lord" and "put all your weight on all of Him!" We can lean on His power, His presence, and His provision.

We find it difficult to trust. Why is that? Is it because it is hard to trust God—who we can't see—with the troubles we can see?

I believe that trust and faith are bound together.

I also believe that the amount of time we spend in worry is in proportion to the amount of faith we have in God. The more faith, the less time we worry. I love what the Lord told Jeremiah: "Behold, I am the LORD, the God of all flesh; is anything too hard for me?" (Jer. 32:27). God is asking the same thing to us today. "Is anything too hard for me?"

Too often, our trust is misplaced like those whom the psalmist described when he wrote, "Some trust in chariots and some in horses" (Ps. 20:7).

Our trust is often misdirected toward the wrong things such as the government, the stock market, education, or to other people such as spouses or friends. The Scriptures, however, repeatedly encourage us to trust in the Lord. Jesus even instructed His disciples just before His departure, "Do not let your hearts be troubled. Trust in God; trust also in me" (John 14:1).

One of the greatest challenges of trusting is that trusting God means we believe what we cannot see. It means *realizing that* God is at work carrying out His purposes even when we do not see evidence of Him working in our lives. "Faith is the confidence that what we hope for will actually happen; it gives us assurance about things we cannot see" (Heb. 11:1, NLT).

Abram had faith to say yes to God's call to travel to an unknown place that would become his home. When he left, he had no idea where he was going. There were no road maps or street signs. By an act of faith, he lived in the country promised him, lived as a stranger camping in tents. "Abraham was confidently loo king forward to a city with eternal foundations, a city designed and built by God" (Heb. 11:10, NLT).

Moses, too, trusted in the invisible. Scripture says when he led the Israelites out of Egypt (Heb. 11:27, NLT), he kept right on going because he kept his eyes on the one who is invisible. Noah's trust in the Lord was amazing. He had no blueprints or building permit. He had never built a boat, nor had he ever seen rain. He was ridiculed by his neighbors. Noah didn't complain or make excuses. He trusted God completely.

Trusting God completely means having faith that he knows what is best for our life. This is true even when we don't understand what is happening to us.

In his book *Trusting God*, Jerry Bridges says, "Trusting God does not mean we do not experience pain. It means that we believe God is at work through the occasion of our pain for ultimate good. It means we work back through the

Scriptures regarding His sovereignty, wisdom, and goodness and ask Him to use those Scriptures to bring peace and comfort to our Hearts....It will often mean that we may have to say, 'God, I don't understand, but I trust You'" (from *The Inspirational Bible*).

Prov. 3:5–6 tells us to "trust in the LORD with all your heart and lean not on your own understanding; in all your ways acknowledge him, and he will make your paths straight."

When we trust God fully, Stan Toler says, "it puts the ball in His court. The pressure is still on—but the pressure is on God, not you. You simply do the daily tasks of life, diligently, faithfully, and skillfully. He's in charge of the bottom line."

Abram did not have a road map nor street sign nor Interstate highways to lead him; all he had was trust.

When called to slay Isaac, his faith was so strong that Abraham believed that if he went through with the sacrifice of Isaac, God would raise Isaac from the dead.

Moses didn't worry about water levels. He simply trusted God to part the waters and get the Israelites through the Red Sea.

Noah did not worry if all would fit, he just built.

Jesus did not worry if the plan of redemption would work or if He would rise again. He trusted in God the Father to work things out. Even when He felt forsaken on the cross, He still trusted the outcome to God.

Do you trust the one whose cross you are called to carry? On a scale of 1 to 10, with 10 being the highest, let me ask you, how strong is your trust in God?

Remember the words of the Lord: "Behold, I am the LORD, the God of all flesh, is anything too hard for me?" (Jer. 32:27).

Part 2: Deny Ourselves

The next step in cross carrying is to deny ourselves.

> Then he said to them all: "If anyone would come after me, he must deny himself and take up his cross daily and follow me. For whoever wants to save his life will lose it, but whoever loses his life for me will save it. What good is it for a man to gain the whole world, and yet lose or forfeit his very self?" (Luke 9:23–25)

Ken Bible: "Because Jesus didn't depend on himself but on His Father, He was free from the fears and struggles of meeting life's challenges on His own strength. He enjoyed a constant rest, a constant peace, a constant sufficiency in His Father."

That's what I want. Don't you? I want that complete peace in Him. When we insist on our own way, we are denying His self and not our self. We then lack the peace, wholeness, and strength that can be ours through Him. We must remember that apart from Jesus, we can do nothing.

> The natural tendency is to save our lives by selfish, complacent, routine, petty existences. We may indulge our pleasures and appetites by basking in comfort, luxury, and ease, by living for the present, by trading our finest talents to the world in exchange for a few years of mock security. But in the very act, we lose our lives, that is, we miss the true purpose of life and the profound spiritual pleasure that should go with it! On the other hand, we may lose our lives for the Savior's sake. Men think us mad if we fling our own selfish ambitions to the wind, if we seek first the kingdom of God and His righteousness, if we yield ourselves unreservedly to Him. But this life of abandonment is genuine living. It has a joy, a holy carefreeness, and a deep inward satisfaction that defies description.[1] (Luke 9:24)

What does it mean to deny myself? I have to give up dependence on my own resources and make myself completely dependent on Jesus's guidance and provision. I have to take my life, comfort, and future out of my own hands and put them totally into His hands. I must trust Jesus to handle everything.

Self-denial does not mean self-rejection. It does not mean wallowing in self-loathing or turning away from everything;

---

1   William MacDonald and Arthur Farstad, *Believer's Bible Commentary: Old and New Testaments* (Nashville: Thomas Nelson, 1997).

you enjoy because "if you like it, it must be bad." Nor is it a diet fad. God "richly provides us with everything for our enjoyment" (1 Tim. 6:17). We know that, far from being worthless, you and I are of infinite value. Jesus thought enough of you to die for you. If He loved you so, how can you hate or reject yourself?

However, denying self is important in discipleship—as long as we understand that it means to *deny everything rooted in the old life*. Deny and reject "the lust of the flesh and the lust of the eyes, and the…pride life" (1 John 2:16, NASB).[2]

> She shouted at her dad. *Oh, how he exasperates me*, she thought. She was mad and let him have it.
>
> She then ran to her room. After the flood of tears, she felt better. She knew she would have to apologize. How she fought making that apology! She told herself it had been his fault—and in some ways, it was. She told herself she *couldn't* go and say, "I'm sorry." Not when *he* should by rights apologize to her first!
>
> Everything in her struggled against the self-humbling that an apology would mean. And for a long time, she stayed in her room, as the tension within her grew.

---

2   Larry Richards and Lawrence O. Richards, *The Teacher's Commentary* (Wheaton: Victor Books, 1987). 668–69.

Finally, Jane got up off her bed and, denying the fears and pride of her old nature, went to do what she knew Jesus wanted. She apologized.

That is self-denial. Cross carrying involves the putting aside our rights that the old self desires and instead live as Jesus would do. A life of Christlikeness requires this kind of denial.

Easy to say, but not easy to do: to disregard my own interest and concern myself only with following Jesus step by step, to focus only on glorifying Him, not myself. It is a process. It's not completed in a moment. It takes time to learn to fully trust Him. There's that word again: *trust*. We are to trust him to take care and command of something very dear and precious to us—ourselves. We must ask the Holy Spirit for his help.

We all face the temptation to control and run our lives—to put ourselves first. That is why we need inside help—the help that can only be ours when we *are filled* with the Holy Spirit.

The key: We must realize that Jesus does not just call us to make a sacrifice. He calls us to be a sacrifice. "Therefore, I urge you, brothers and sisters, in view of God's mercy, to offer your bodies as a living sacrifice, holy and pleasing to God—this is your true and proper worship (Rom. 12:1, NIV). He calls us to full devotion to and dependence on him. The cross calls us to total dedication, not halfhearted commitment.

When we deny ourselves, we are making room for Him to truly come alive in us. What a wonderful trade. Our self for His self.

Part 3: In Public

In part 1 of our study, we dealt with trusting God. Part 2 dealt with denying ourselves. Now, I will explain what I believe it means to carry our cross in public.

> Then he said to them all: "If anyone would come after me, he must deny himself and take up his cross daily and follow me. For whoever wants to save his life will lose it, but whoever loses his life for me will save it. What good is it for a man to gain the whole world, and yet lose or forfeit his very self?" (Luke 9:23–25)
> When I read our passage for the first time, I pictured a scene much like the one below. I do not like showing off in public and was hoping that this is not what Jesus meant.

I believe that taking up our cross means to see everyone through the eyes of Jesus. To see everyone through the eyes of Jesus, we are going to need to be reminded that Jesus saw everyone through the eyes of love. I picture taking up my cross this way; imagine that you have a cross like the one pictured below. It is clear in the middle, so when I hold it up to my face, I can see through it.

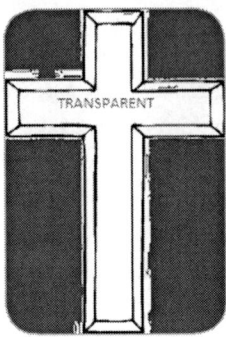

What does it mean to take up your cross? It means that we must see each other through the cross of Jesus. Colossians 3:1–3, 8–10 share some guidelines:

> If then you have been raised up with Christ, keep seeking the things above, where Christ is, seated at the right hand of God. Set your mind on the things above, not on the things that are on earth. For you have died and your life is hidden with Christ in God. (NASB)

But now you also, put them all aside: anger, wrath, malice, slander, and abusive speech from your mouth. Do not lie to one another, since you laid aside the old self with its evil practices, and have put on the new self who is being renewed to a true knowledge according to the image of the One who created him. And so, as those who have been chosen of God, holy and beloved, put on a heart of compassion, kindness, humility, gentleness and patience; bearing with one another, and forgiving each other, whoever has a complaint against anyone; just as the Lord forgave you, so also should you. And beyond all these things put on love, which is the perfect bond of unity. And whatever you do in word or deed, do all in the name of the Lord Jesus, giving thanks through Him to God the Father.

Everything that we do must be filtered through that "see-through" cross.

"Set your mind" (verse 2). Look through your cross.

"Life is hidden" (verse 8). Look through your cross.

"Put aside" (verse 8). Look through your cross.

"Lay aside" (verse 9). Look through your cross.

"Put on" (verse 10). Look through your cross.

"Bearing and forgiving" (verse 13). Look through your cross.

"Put on love" (verse 14). Look through your cross.

"And whatever you do in word or deed, do all in the name of the Lord Jesus, giving thanks through Him to God the Father." Look through your cross.

I wonder what effect using the see-through cross could have on our family dynamics ,your church.

What could happen to your workplace when you realize it was Jesus who you were really working for?

How would the world be if every Christian saw the world through the see-through cross? It makes one wonder, doesn't it?

Part 4: Grin and Bear It?

I believe that carrying our cross can also refer to some kind of affliction, burden, a problem, or hardship. I will explain: You could have a demanding boss in a stressful job, or a child who is not doing what they should be doing, or it could be Parkinson's or cancer—any of those are crosses to bear. Think of cross carrying being another name for the hard times that we will undergo.

It will be easier to carry our crosses upright and not drag them behind as long as we remember:

We do not have to carry our cross alone.

Billy Graham says, "Nowhere does the Bible teach that Christians are exempt from the tribulations and natural disasters that come upon the world. Scripture does teach that the Christian can face tribulation, crisis, calamity, and personal suffering with a supernatural power that is not available to the person outside of Christ."

There is a power that is available to us if we will ask—the power of the Holy Spirit. The same power that raised Jesus from the dead can be ours.

One of my most favorite hymn writers is Horatio G. Spafford. His four-year-old son, Horatio Jr., died of scarlet fever. The Spaffords were devastated.

In October of 1871, one year later, when the Great Chicago Fire broke out, Horatio faced another test of his faith. A few months before the Great Fire, Spafford had invested most of his wealth in real estate by the shore of Lake Michigan. Not only did the Great Chicago Fire destroy most of Chicago but most of Spafford's holdings were destroyed also.

If that was not a big enough cross to carry, his wife and daughters took a cruise. On the way to their destination, the cruise ship was struck by another and sank in twenty minutes, killing all four of his daughters.

Upon hearing the terrible news, Spafford boarded a ship to meet his wife. On the Atlantic crossing, the captain of his ship called Horatio to his cabin to tell him that they were passing over the spot where his four daughters had died. Spafford felt the comfort and inspiration of the Holy Spirit as he wrote:

When peace, like a river, attendeth my way,
When sorrows like sea billows roll;
Whatever my lot, thou hast taught me to say,
It is well, it is well with my soul.

It is well with my soul;
It is well, it is well with my soul.

Though Satan should buffet, though trials should come,
Let this blest assurance control,
That Christ has regarded my helpless estate,
And has shed his own blood for my soul.

My sin—O the bliss of this glorious thought!—
My sin, not in part, but the whole,
Is nailed to the cross and I bear it no more;
Praise the Lord, praise the Lord, O my soul!

O Lord, haste the day when the faith shall be sight,
The clouds be rolled back as a scroll,
The trump shall resound and the Lord shall descend;
"Even so"—it is well with my soul.

How could someone go through so much hardship and still carry his cross up right and not drag it behind? There is no way that we can face such horrible events without the power offered to us by the Holy Spirit.

The natural tendency of one confronted with such senseless tragedy would surely be to question, to doubt, to blame, to accuse God, and even reject God. Yet this hymn reveals a person who had been empowered by God to mourn without bitterness, to sorrow without anger, to trust without resentment, to rest in the peace of Christ, which surpasses every man's understanding (Phil. 4:6). The secret is to let the Holy Spirit carry your cross.

Meditate on these words:

> Be strong and courageous. Do not be afraid or terrified because of the LORD your God goes with you; he will never leave you nor forsake you. (Deut. 31:6, NIV)

> No one will be able to stand up against you all the days of your life. As I was with Moses, so I will be with you; I will never leave you nor forsake you. (Josh. 1:5, NIV)

> "Never will I leave you; never will I forsake you." (Heb. 13:5, NIV)

God is with us in our darkest hour. He promises us that He will never leave us nor forsake us. He offers to us His presence and His power.

> But now, this is what the LORD says—he who created you, O Jacob, he who formed you, O Israel: "Fear not, for I have redeemed you; I have summoned you by name; you are mine. When you pass through the waters, I will be with you; and when you pass through the rivers, they will not sweep over you. When you

walk through the fire, you will not be burned; the flames will not set you ablaze. For I am the LORD, your God, the Holy One of Israel, your Savior. (Isa. 43:1–3)

Tragedies and hard times are always agonizing and often senseless. Praise God that we do not have to carry the cross without help.

I cannot imagine what it would be like to endure a tragedy—to carry the cross—without the hope that God offers. Without Jesus Christ, there is no hope.

Jesus says, "Come to Me, all who are weary and heavy-laden, and I will give you rest. 'Take My yoke upon you and learn from Me, for I am gentle and humble in heart, and YOU WILL FIND REST FOR YOUR SOULS.' For My yoke is easy and My burden is light" (Matt. 11:28–30, NASB).

Sanctification—What It Ain't

> May God himself, the God of peace, sanctify you through and through. May your whole spirit, soul and body be kept blameless at the coming of our Lord Jesus Christ. The one who calls you is faithful and he will do it. (1 Thess. 5:23–24)

SANCTIFICATION—HEART HOLINESS—IS A misunderstood theory among Christians. Some feel that it is a one-shot deal given at salvation. The Church of the Nazarene teaches that it comes after salvation and is a crisis experience. It is the power to love the unlovable. Let's look at some of the myths:

Falsehood 1: Sanctification will allow me to live in constant communion with God throughout the day.

I know of people who have claimed that God has told them what to do every day. He even tells them what they should eat for lunch. They even know what God says I should do before He even tells me. (They are not correct, most of the time.)

I wonder if they have a special hotline to God.

As a sanctified believer, you will still experience dry seasons and times when it will seem as though God has left you. Total commitment to God does not keep us from feeling disconnected at times. That's when blind trust in the promise that He is always with us comes in.

Falsehood 2: The minute God sanctified me, I became bold, outgoing, and confident.

Holiness does not immediately change your personality type. I wish it did. We could all solve our personality problems in a moment. I have heard people tell how their commitment to God revolutionized their personality to the point that they hardly believed the different person they instantly became. Nevertheless, it doesn't happen that way for most of us. An extrovert will still have plenty to say to the stranger in the grocery store checkout line. An introvert will still tend to hide in the shadows at the back of the room. Yes, we will receive the power to be a witness for Christ; however, not many of us will receive the bravery to stand on the street corner and preach like Peter did in the book of Acts.

Falsehood 3: I used to have mood swings, but not since I got sanctified. No more highs and lows for me, thank God!

What kind of pills are these people taking? Holiness does not change your basic temperament. Jeremiah still wept, Paul still got mad, and Jesus still got depressed.

Some look on the dark side of every situation and have a tendency toward negative thoughts. Some see the glass half full rather than half empty. Others see the glass half empty with a hole in it. We don't suddenly begin to act in unusual new ways.

Each one of the disciples still had their own personality even though they were Spirit-filled. God will help us become more like Him, but it will take time.

Falsehood 4: Since I gave everything to God, I don't get discouraged.

Discouragement has many causes. It's seldom a matter of spiritual weakness.

It can result from a physical or mental illness, from disappointment over bad news or a personal failure.

Jesus got discouraged.

"To say once we are sanctified we never get discouraged forces conscientious followers of Christ to hide their natural responses to life's downturns. Some of the most godly saints in the Bible and church history experienced discouragement— some severe depression. We may become discouraged too" (Moore).

Falsehood 5: Since God sanctified me. I have become immune to temptation.

This is a common misunderstanding about holiness. David was filled with the Spirit, and look what he did with Bathsheba.

There are some in the church who say, "I am sanctified; therefore, I am without sin and cannot fall."

Eradication of the sinful nature used to be preached by Nazarene pastors.

> So, if you think you are standing firm, be careful that you don't fall! (1 Cor. 10:12)

> If we claim to be without sin, we deceive ourselves and the truth is not in us. (1 John 1:8)

Holiness does not end the possibility for temptation or sin. Study the Scriptures. All the saints in the Bible resisted temptation. Temptation even knocked at Jesus's door. What sanctification does, however, is give you greater strength against temptation.

We never give up our right to sin. We never lose our free will.

Falsehood 6: Since I am sanctified, life will be a bed of roses.

> For it has been granted to you on behalf of Christ not only to believe on him, but also to suffer for him. (Phil. 1:29)

We are not immune from hardship or hard times; they are a part of life. We will suffer.

Falsehood 7: Holiness solved all my problems of anger.

"Nothing ever frustrates or stresses me since the Holy Spirit took control." I wish.

Holiness does not instantly change the way we react when frustrated or provoked. We will still go through stressful situations when we are Spirit-filled.

We are all exposed to annoyances, some more annoying than others. Sometimes they will get the best of us and we will react. This is a normal response. Anger turned inward can lead to depression and rage.

Anger uncontrolled can hurt and harm. Anger that is controlled by the Holy Spirit is healthy.

We must ask the Holy Spirit to help us with our anger if it is a problem. Someone wrote, "He that strives not to stem his anger's tide does a wild horse without a bridle ride."

Falsehood 8: Holiness replaced all my desires for material possessions with spiritual goals.

> On the surface this sounds virtuous. However, followed to its logical conclusion, it makes little sense. A young friend of mine once made this claim then shared with me his plans for the future. He planned to quit his job, sell his car, move out of his apartment, and pursue only spiritual concerns. I never understood

how he could live without income or a roof over his head, but he sounded extremely spiritual. He now sells lumber.

A life of holiness does not disqualify you from earning an income or owning a home, car, and personal possessions. It does mean you must be a responsible steward of your money and possessions.

It means pursuing a balanced life of work and relaxation. It means living within your means so that your house and car payments do not control your life. It means *not* defining your personhood or worth by your possessions. And it means not letting material possessions come between you and God or His call on your life. So, can we escape all association with material possessions to pursue only spiritual goals? Not likely.

Falsehood 9: Now that I'm sanctified, I no longer struggle with doubts or fears about anything in life.

> A pastor told this story: One Sunday a few years ago, while teaching my Sunday school class, I led the group in discussing the doubts and fears that sometimes plague Christians. We talked about fear of tornadoes, inner-city gangs, big dogs, mountain cliffs, and spiders.
>
> We talked about doubts of whether we'd said the right thing in a particular situation, responded to our children appropriately, or had done all we knew to

do for God. We also talked about the questions that run through our minds when we're going through the dark valleys of life. Questions like, "Where is God?" "Is He listening to my prayers?" "Does He even care about the situation I'm in right now?"

One dear older saint of the class said, "I'm not comfortable with this discussion. I do not think holiness people will ever experience any kind of doubt or fear if they are truly filled with the Holy Spirit."

What can you say after that? She played the "highly spiritual" card. I tried to show how these types of doubts, fears, and questions are a normal part of life, even a sanctified believer's life. I don't think I convinced her of my position.

I strongly believe holiness does not calm all our doubts and fears about life. Many things in life remain uncertain. However, sanctification does not dehumanize us. If you didn't like spiders as a sinner, you probably won't like them as a saint.

I like the way G. Campbell Morgan summarized the results of being sanctified.

1. Not inability to sin, but ability not to sin
2. Not freedom from temptation, but power to overcome temptation
3. Not deliverance from infirmities of the flesh, but triumph over all bodily affliction

4. Not exemption from conflict, but victory through conflict
5. Not freedom from falling, but the ability to prevent falling

> May God himself, the God of peace, sanctify you through and through. May your whole spirit, soul and body be kept blameless at the coming of our Lord Jesus Christ. The one who calls you is faithful and he will do it. (1 Thess. 5:23–24)

While sanctification doesn't free us from temptation, discouragement, stress, or mood swings, it does enable us to be more Christlike. Wouldn't you like that power?

God Became Flesh

W<small>E</small> <small>MUST NOT</small> forget that Jesus was fully human and fully God. Isaiah 53:2–3 tells us that Jesus was not very good-looking.

> He grew up before him like a tender shoot, and like a root out of dry ground. He had no beauty or majesty to attract us to him, nothing in his appearance that we should desire him. He was despised and rejected by men, a man of sorrows, and familiar with suffering. Like one from whom men hide their faces he was despised, and we esteemed him not. (Isa. 53:2–3, NIV)

There was nothing about his appearance that was at all attention getting. He had red hair and a big nose. His large hands were calloused. His face was weathered from the desert sun—skin like sandpaper. He was tall and muscular.

Whenever He spoke, he attracted a crowd. His words were mesmerizing to some, irritating to others, *puzzling* and aggravating to the rest.

He was a master storyteller who would hold your attention to the very end, and then you would find yourself asking for more. His speeches were somewhat weird sometimes: "The meek shall inherit...him who wants to save his life will lose it...the first shall be last."

> Whoever eats my flesh and drinks my blood has eternal life, and I will raise them up at the last day. (John 6:54)

He rarely ate alone. He loved to grill and especially enjoyed eating with the poor and the "down and outs." He had a knack for making them feel welcome. My, how he loved a good, clean joke. There were times that he would be laughing so hard that his eyes would water. His friends were thieves, prostitutes, tax collectors, and other misfits.

Children were extremely important to Him. He would always take time to play a few minutes with them.

His personality was like a Tootsie Roll Pop—hard on the outside and soft on the inside. He did not hide his emotions. He got down right mad at the moneychangers in the temple (some may call it righteous indignation—I will call it anger [torked off?]). He wept when his friend Lazarus died. He felt sadness when Judas betrayed Him; he was frustrated with his disciples when they would bicker with each other. He was passionate when He went about doing *his Father's* business. His love held Him on the cross.

He was compassionate, kind, and gentle; and at the same time, he was tough. Those pictures that show an effeminate Jesus are terrible distortions of the truth. He was a carpenter—rugged and solidly built.

He loved a good nap. He even had those days when he would measure twice, and the board would still be too short.

When he was to announce who he was, he rode into town on a donkey instead of a horse. What a strange way to announce his kingship. His compassion got to Him as he was overlooking the crowd. He—instead of being overjoyed with their praises and hosannas—wept. Was it the fickleness of the crowd?

His last few weeks were tough—to say the least; he was being harassed by the religious establishment (the scribes, the Pharisees, the teachers of the law). A warrant was issued for his arrest. He was in trouble because he said "I AM"—God's holy name. He was arrested and illegally tried in an illegal court (he was a blasphemer). Courts could not meet at night, and there had to be two collaborating witnesses. There was none, and he was declared guilty.

He—full of love—was attacked by those full of hate. Whipped, mocked, spat upon, bloodied, weakened, thirsty, betrayed, stripped naked, humiliated, crucified. Full of love, he cried out, "Father, forgive them. They do not know what they are doing."

More humiliation, more pain; the sinless became sin—took on our sins—he shouted, "My God, why have you forsaken me?"

Immanuel—God in the flesh—descended into hell—that's where sinners go. And then he did something so wonderful: he rose from the grave and is alive today! And as a result, he offers us eternal life.

> For God so loved the world that he gave his one and only Son, that whoever believes in Him shall not perish but have eternal life. Jesus said to her, "I am the resurrection and the life. He who believes in me will live, even though he dies; and whoever lives and believes in me will never die. (John 3:16, NIV)

I need to ask you a very important question: Do you believe in Jesus?

> If you declare with your mouth, "Jesus is Lord," and believe in your heart that God raised Him from the dead, you will be saved. For it is with your heart that you believe and are justified, and it is with your mouth that you profess your faith and are saved. (Rom. 10:9–10, NIV)

Go Tell Peter

I'M GOING TO do a little role-playing I am going to attempt to see things through the eyes of Peter.

I still remember that week as if the events had happened yesterday. There in the Garden of Gethsemane, Jesus was alone. Judas had made his move. James, John, and I could not stay awake.

I was there as He was captured. There was a large crowd armed with swords and clubs. I stood aside as I watched Judas approach Jesus. He went right up to him and kissed the Lord. The scene sickened me:

> Going at once to Jesus, Judas said, "Greetings, Rabbi!" and kissed him. Jesus replied, "Friend, do what you came for." Then the men stepped forward, seized Jesus and arrested him. (Matt. 26:49–50)

As soon as they seized him, I took out my sword and cut off the ear of the high priest's servant.

I'll never forget the Lord's words:

> "Put your sword back in its place," Jesus said to him, "for all who draw the sword will die by the sword. Do you think I cannot call on my Father, and he will at once put at my disposal more than twelve legions of angels? But how then would the Scriptures be fulfilled that say it must happen in this way?" (Matt. 26:52–54)

I watched as they took him to Caiaphas, the high priest. I even sat with the guards and talked to them, pretending not to know Jesus. I listened attentively to the questioning of the high priest. "Are you the Christ, the son of the living God?" he asked.

> "Yes, it is as you say," Jesus replied. "But I say to all of you: In the future you will see the Son of Man sitting at the right hand of the Mighty One and coming on the clouds of heaven." Then the high priest tore his clothes and said, "He has spoken blasphemy! Why do we need any more witnesses? Look, now you have heard the blasphemy." (Matt. 26:64–65)

They then sentenced him to death. I watched as they spat on him and slapped him. Why didn't he do anything? Why did he just take it? Could it be that he really was God?

A servant girl recognized me. Then I—the same disciple who had vowed that, if necessary, would die for Christ—now three times in succession, vehemently denied knowing Jesus. The Master had predicted that this would happen.

The rooster crowed, and I was immediately filled with shame and remorse. I, like Judas, had betrayed my best friend. I ran outside and wept bitterly.

Judas watched as Jesus was tied up—as a common criminal—and realized that he had blown it. He ran and hung himself on a tree. All I could do was cry.

Then Jesus was brought to Pontius Pilate, the governor. He asked Jesus if he was the king of the Jews. Jesus simply said, "Yes, it is as you say."

He was then accused by the chief priests and the religious elite and didn't even say a word. Nothing. Pilate was frustrated. Hoping to appease them, he offered to release either Barabbas or Jesus—hoping that they would choose Jesus, as Barabbas was a notorious criminal.

Listen to what happened as my friend Matthew wrote about it:

> But the chief priests and the elders persuaded the crowd to ask for Barabbas and to have Jesus executed. "Which of the two do you want me to release to you?" asked the governor. "Barabbas," they answered. "What shall I do, then, with Jesus who is called Christ?" Pilate asked. They all answered, "Crucify him!"

"Why? What crime has he committed?" asked Pilate. But they shouted all the louder, "Crucify him!" When Pilate saw that he was getting nowhere, but that instead an uproar was starting, he took water and washed his hands in front of the crowd. "I am innocent of this man's blood," he said. "It is your responsibility!" All the people answered, "Let his blood be on us and on our children!" Then he released Barabbas to them. But he had Jesus flogged, and handed him over to be crucified. (Matt. 27:20–26)

It was rather strange seeing the same people praising him on Sunday and cursing him a few days later.

I watched as they took Jesus to the *praetorium*; they stripped him, put a scarlet robe on him, and pounded a crown of thorns onto his head. Then they put a staff in his hands and mocked him. Then they spat on him and struck him on the head again and again. I watched as he began to bleed. Then they led him away to be crucified.

I can still hear the mocking of the crowd, "He saved others, let him save himself. You are God? Prove it. What a king. Crucify him and get it over with."

Life had come down to this—dying on a cross.

No glory.

Just dying.

Jesus, who had raised Lazarus from the dead, now refused to save himself. The One who had forgiven hundreds now suffered between thieves. The Messiah, who had been God's presence for so many, now cried out, "My God, my God, why have you forsaken me?" (verse 46). Finally, Jesus gave up His spirit.

He quit breathing.

His heart stopped beating.

He died.

> And behold,[1] the veil[2] of the temple was torn in two from top to bottom;[3] and the earth shook and the rocks were split.[4] The tombs were opened, and many bodies of the saints[5] who had fallen asleep were raised;[6] and coming out of the tombs after His resurrection they entered the holy city and appeared to many.[7] Now the centurion,[8] and those who were with him keeping guard over Jesus, when they saw[9] the earthquake and the things that were happening, became very frightened and said, "Truly this was the Son of God!"[10] (Matt. 27:51–54, NASB)

---

1 Matt. 27:51–56, Mark 15:38–41, Luke 23:47–49

2 or *curtain*

3 Exod. 26:31ff, Mark 15:38, Luke 23:45, Heb. 9:3

4 Matt. 27:54

5 or *holy ones*

6 Acts 7:60

7 Matt. 4:5

8 Mark 15:39, Luke 23:47

9 Matt. 27:36

10 Matt. 4:3, 27:43; or "a son of God" / "a son of a God"

Then came Sunday—the greatest day in history had dawned. It began sadly though. Two women, both named Mary, traveled to the tomb to pay their last respects. Suddenly, the ground began to shake, and an angel appeared. Walking past guards who had fainted from fear, the two women accepted the angel's invitation to see where Jesus had lain. The tomb was open! The angel reminded them of Jesus's promise that He would rise from the dead. He then said, "Go tell the disciples and go tell Peter." Yes, go tell *me*—the one who had betrayed him. What love. What grace. What an amazing God. I had betrayed him three times, and I'm forgiven—what amazing grace! He forgave me! Yes, me.

Hallelujah, What a Savior

"Man of Sorrows!" What a name
For the Son of God, who came
Ruined sinners to reclaim.
Hallelujah! What a Savior!

Bearing shame and scoffing rude,
In my place condemned He stood;
Sealed my pardon with His blood.
Hallelujah! What a Savior!

Guilty, vile, and helpless we;
Spotless Lamb of God was He;
"Full atonement!" can it be?
Hallelujah! What a Savior!

Lifted up was He to die;
"It is finished!" was His cry;
Now in Heav'n exalted high.
Hallelujah! What a Savior!
     When He comes, our glorious King,
All His ransomed home to bring,
Then anew His song we'll sing:
Hallelujah! What a Savior!

The Loving Father

ONE OF THE greatest examples of God's love, grace, and forgiveness is found in the story of the Prodigal Son.

> Jesus continued: "There was a man who had two sons.
>
> "The younger one said to his Father, 'Father, give me my share of the estate.' So he divided his property between them. Not long after that, the younger son got together all he had, set off for a distant country and there squandered his wealth in wild living. After he had spent everything, there was a severe famine in that whole country, and he began to be in need. So he went and hired himself out to a citizen of that country, who sent him to his fields to feed pigs. He longed to fill his stomach with the pods that the pigs were eating, but no one gave him anything. When he came to his senses, he said, 'How many of my Father's hired men have food to spare, and here I am starving to death!

'I will set out and go back to my Father and say to him: "Father, I have sinned against heaven and against you. I am no longer worthy to be called your son; make me like one of your hired men."' So he got up and went to his Father. But while he was still a long way off, his Father saw him and was filled with compassion for him; he ran to his son, threw his arms around him and kissed him. The son said to him, 'Father, I have sinned against heaven and against you. I am no longer worthy to be called your son.' But the Father said to his servants, 'Quick! Bring the best robe and put it on him. Put a ring on his finger and sandals on his feet. Bring the fattened calf and kill it. Let's have a feast and celebrate. For this son of mine was dead and is alive again; he was lost and is found.' So they began to celebrate. Meanwhile, the older son was in the field. When he came near the house, he heard music and dancing, so he called one of the servants and asked him what was going on. 'Your brother has come,' he replied, 'and your Father has killed the fattened calf because he has him back safe and sound.' The older brother became angry and refused to go in. So his Father went out and pleaded with him. But he answered his Father, 'Look! All these years I've been slaving for you and never disobeyed your orders. Yet you never gave me even a young goat so I could celebrate with my friends. But when this son of yours who has squandered your property with prostitutes comes home, you kill the fattened calf for him!'

'My son,' the Father said, 'you are always with me, and everything I have is yours. But we had to celebrate and be glad, because this brother of yours was dead and is alive again; he was lost and is found.'" (Luke 15:11–32, NIV)

Yacov—the Prodigal Son—woke up one day and began to look around at the vast estate. There were the pens of cattle, sheep, and goats; miles and miles of grape arbors; and row after row of olive trees. He walked around the servant quarters that held hundreds of servants.

To the north end of the property was the giant, many-roomed mansion that he lived in. He had his own horse and custom-made buggy and his own camels. Yacov was an impeccable dresser. His shirts were of the finest material. His pants were custom fitted; his boots cost more than a year's salary. He was healthy, wealthy, but not so wise.

He quietly checked around and got the latest update on his family's net worth and then figured that a third of it—as he is the second son—was his correct inheritance, according to the law. *Wow! If I would ask for my inheritance now, I'll be rich. Think of the great time that I'll be able to have with a ton of money.*

Slowly he mustered his courage, as greed got to him, and finally he faced his dad.

"Dad," he says.

"Yes, son."

"Dad, I want my inheritance."

"Sure, son, one day you'll have it."

"No, Dad, I want it now."

Slowly and reluctantly, the dad responds, "Are you sure? You want it now?"

"Yes, Dad, now."

"Do you understand the consequences?"

"Yes, Dad, I do."

There are two occasions that require drastic measures in the life of a Jew. They are so drastic that the law requires a funeral to be held and then all future relationships with the person are prohibited. They are when a Jew converts to Christianity and when a Jewish son asks for his inheritance before the death of the father.

The dad reluctantly agrees and goes to the bank and withdraws the proper amount from the company's account. He hands the son the money and says good-bye.

The son packs his belongings, hitches up his favorite horse, and heads for the distant city. He hears that they have a lot of action there.

He arrives in the distant city, eyes bright as saucers as he looks around at all the glitter. He begins to flash a little money and finds that he begins attracting "friends." He parties heavy and begins buying rounds of drinks for his friends. They meet night after night, and he is always furnishing the liquor.

His friends can't keep up with the fast pace of his partying and slowly leave him. He continues partying, and one day, he wakes up and realizes that he just has enough money for one last meal and to pay for his room.

He checks out and looks for his friends. The word has gotten out that he is broke, and they want nothing to do with him. He is hungry and needs money.

He hastily writes out a resume on some papyrus and begins passing it out. A pig farmer reads his resume and hires him to feed the pigs. He is so hungry that the pig slop looks good to him. As a Jew, he could have stooped no lower. He had hit rock bottom.

He is covered with mud and pig slop, his boots are ruined, he hasn't had a shower in weeks. Slowly he comes to his senses and realizes that his own father's servants had it better than he does. He decides to go back to his father and work for him. Surely he would be better off to work for his father than for a foreigner.

He composes his apology and begins the long journey home.

As he enters the gates to the estate, he begins practicing his apology. He passes through the gates and starts down the long road to his house. His father is outside on the porch, looks up, and sees his son in the distance.

The father runs toward him and gives him a giant bear hug and kisses him. Before he can finish his carefully rehearsed apology, the father interrupts and yells to his servants, "Quick, bring out the best clothes, a new pair of shoes, and the family ring. Prepare the beef, and let's party, my son is home."

What an amazing story.

What an example of love.

The theologian William Barclay says, "For centuries the parable has been called 'The Parable of the Prodigal Son.' It would be far better if we were to call it 'The Parable of the Loving Father' for it is the Father and not the son who is the hero of the story."

This parable shows us what God is really like. We can learn several things about God. It truly is a love story.

1. The Father lets us have our way.

   When the son went to his father and asked for his inheritance, he was saying that he no longer wanted to be under his father's authority. He wanted to have his fling and sow his wild oats.

   There is no indication in our Scriptures that the dad argues with the son or tried to talk him out of it.

   This is the same freedom that God gives us. We have the free will to choose to serve him or not. We have the right and privilege of sinning if we want to.

   This is *not* his will, of course. But he will let us go if we want.

   We never give up our free will or the right to sin.

2. The Father waits for our return.

   Our Scriptures imply that the father each day would look down the long entrance to his estate with the hopes that the son would return. That is the picture we have of God waiting for us to return to him. Even though the son was out of sight, he was never out of his dad's heart.

> So he got up and went to his Father. But while he was still a long way off, his Father saw him and was filled with compassion for him; he ran to his son, threw his arms around him and kissed him. (Luke 15:20, NIV)

What a wonderful God. This is one of the rare times that we ever see God in a hurry. When we come back to him, he runs toward us.

The incredible thing is that the picture is the same if we are coming to God for the first time. He is there waiting for us and will run toward us.

3. The Father grants us forgiveness.

It did not matter to the father what the son had done. What was important was that the son began to confess his sins.

> If we confess our sins, he is faithful and just and will forgive us our sins and purify us from all unrighteousness. (1 John 1:9, NIV)

God's grace is free and is available to all. There is no sin too horrible, no person too evil that can't be forgiven if only he'll ask.

The father would not even listen to all of the young son's rehearsed speech. Instead, the father had his servants prepare a banquet to celebrate the son's return.

He shouts, "My son was dead and is now alive. He was lost and now is found!"

Remember, when a Jewish son asks for his inheritance before the death of the father, the father grants the son's wish and then has a funeral for the son. Hence, he was dead.

The father was filled with grace and love. Al Truesdale wrote: "Grace. There is no sweeter word in any language. And there is no grander word in all the theological books of the world." God's love is gracious. God's grace is loving.

4. The Father's love celebrates our return.

When the son returned, and began to repent, the father celebrated his return by throwing a party.

> I tell you, there is rejoicing in the presence of the angels of God over one sinner who repents. (Luke 15:31, NIV)

"But we had to celebrate and be glad, because this brother of yours was dead and is alive again; he was lost and is found."

5. The Father's love restores.

The son did not ask to be restored to his rightful place as a son. He was willing to be treated as one of his father's employees. He had completely underestimated his Father's love.

Love, which drove him to look for his son each and every day.

Love, which ran to meet him.

Love, which interrupted his son's confession.

Love, which restored him to his rightful place.

He was not only restored as son, he was given a party, new shoes, and the family ring. On it was a seal, and wherever it was presented, the merchant would give unlimited credit, like an American Express card without a limit; this further showed that the son was fully restored.

That is the way God treats us when we confess our sins. He wipes the slate clean and restores us. It is called justification, which means "Just as if I didn't do it." What a wonderful Lord.

He then restores us to our place as sons and daughters of the King.

What an amazing God!

He gives us freedom, waits for us to come to him, forgives us, wipes the slate clean, celebrates and restores us.

My Savior's Love

I stand amazed in the presence
Of Jesus the Nazarene.
And wonder how He could love me,
A sinner, condemned, unclean.

How marvelous! How wonderful!
And my song shall ever be:
How marvelous, how wonderful
Is my Savior's love for me!

For me it was in the garden
He prayed "Not My will but Thine."
He had no tears for His own grief,
But sweat drops of blood for mine.
How marvelous! How wonderful!
And my song shall ever be:
How marvelous, how wonderful
Is my Savior's love for me!

In pity angels behold Him,
And came from the world of light
To comfort Him in the sorrows
He bore for my soul that night.

How marvelous! How wonderful!
And my song shall ever be:
How marvelous, how wonderful
Is my Savior's love for me!

He took my sins and my sorrows;
He made them His very own;
He bore the burden to Calvary,
And suffered and died alone.

How marvelous! How wonderful!
And my song shall ever be:
How marvelous, how wonderful
Is my Savior's love for me!

When with the ransomed in glory
His face I at last shall see,
'Twill be my joy through the ages
To sing of His love for me.
How marvelous! How wonderful!
And my song shall ever be:
How marvelous, how wonderful
Is my Savior's love for me!

CPSIA information can be obtained
at www.ICGtesting.com
Printed in the USA
FSOW02n1039100916
24780FS